PRAISE FOR

The Get Ready! Blueprint

"*The Get Ready! Blueprint: A 52-Week Guide to Changing the Way You Think About Money* is a must-read for anyone who wants to take control of their financial future. Tony's practical approach is refreshing and non-judgmental, helping readers to create healthy financial habits that work for them. This planner is a comprehensive guide that not only provides a road map to financial independence but also encourages readers to understand their values, expectations, and communication around money, ultimately leading to a lifetime of financial preparedness and peace of mind."

—CHIHEE KIM, co-founder and co-CEO, Finny

"Financial ideals connect with action in *The Get Ready! Blueprint* by Tony Steuer. In his new book, Steuer inspires weekly goal setting and execution through a series of well-considered prompts—from assembling an advisory team to verifying you're on track to financial independence. Follow Tony's lead to get ready and stay ready."

—JULIE RAINS, author of *Growing Wealth: Essential Money Lessons from My Garden to Yours*

"*The Get Ready! Blueprint: A 52-Week Guide to Changing the Way You Think About Money* is a practical road map that empowers consumers to create healthy financial habits that align with their individual values, priorities, and passions. Tony has curated essential information, forms, and checklists to help individuals, couples, and families create and maintain healthy money habits for life. (This guide will transform how we think about money and start a movement!)"

—MARGUERITA CHENG, CFP® and chief executive officer, Blue Ocean Global Wealth

"It's all here. Everything you need to get your personal finances in place is in *The Get Ready! Blueprint*. From realistic time schedules to step-by-step plans to easy-to-understand financial guidance, it's all here. The only thing missing from this financial formula for success is the reader's desire to want to be better with their money. If you want to better manage your finances and if you are looking for the complete package, there are no better books on the market to bring everything together in one place. It's all here!"

—MAC GARDNER, CFP®, founder and chief education officer, FinLit Tech

"Having known Tony for years and having had the pleasure of collaborating with him on an article on financial wellness, I applaud him for taking on the task of educating the audience on building healthy money habits from a process and temperament perspective. His weekly money planner keeps the reader frequently on track with their financial goals, and action steps are constantly being addressed as part of daily living and not a dreaded must-do when it is after the fact and probably painful. I applaud Tony for his ongoing and vigilant work in the insurance and financial services industry and for creating an easy-to-read work plan that can be shared with family members and caretakers. Well done, Tony!"

—KEENA PETTIJOHN, founder and CEO, Lifelogixs

THE GET *Ready!* Blueprint

A 52-Week Guide to Changing the Way You Think About Money

TONY STEUER, CLU, LA, CPFFE

LIFE
INSURANCE
SAGE
PRESS

Published by Life Insurance Sage Press
Alameda, CA
tonysteuer.com

Distributed by River Grove Books

Design and composition by Greenleaf Book Group
Cover design by Greenleaf Book Group

Publisher's Cataloging-in-Publication data is available.

Print ISBN: 978-1-7342100-6-4
eBook ISBN: 978-1-7342100-7-1

First Edition

Contents

Introduction

Over the years, people have asked me about all sorts of things about their money. While the questions can be tactical in nature, such as how to choose their employee benefits or allocate their investments, the underlying questions are *How do I take care of my family?* and *Will I have enough money to reach financial independence?* The questions are about subjective goals rather than objective product analysis.

This is a big disconnect. When we think about our money, we are trying to meet a goal or solve a problem. However, we often get sidetracked by thinking about the product first rather than thinking about whether it fits into our financial lives and will help us meet our goals. Think about it like this: When you go grocery shopping, you usually have a list. A lot of this list is based on recipes you plan to make that week. You buy the items to make that dish. So, if you are planning to make spaghetti and meatballs, you probably wouldn't buy smoked salmon. You would be focused on the dish. However, when we go shopping for financial products, we often start with the product first, ending up with a bunch of disparate products that we try to make into one of our financial recipes (a goal such as financial independence). Why are we trying to squeeze smoked salmon into our spaghetti and meatballs?

There are endless books that tell you how to do a specific task like set up a budget, save for retirement, and invest your money. And there are also books that help you think about things like the psychology of money. And then there are the books and financial gurus who tell you all of the things that you're doing wrong.

What's missing is a method that helps you create healthy financial habits that put you in charge, that provides a roadmap, and that is nonjudgmental. It's not about decisions that you've made in the past, it's about what you do moving forward. And there's nothing wrong with getting the occasional grande decaf cappuccino with coconut milk at Starbucks (my current favorite drink). Instead of worrying about a $5 decision, focus on the $1,000 decisions, such as saving 1 percent in annual expenses on a $100,000 mutual fund investment. Those savings would buy you 200 lattes at $5 a pop.

This planner is all about helping you understand who you are and what you want to accomplish and then guiding you to make your own decisions with clear action steps. You'll gain an overall view of how everything fits together and then how to maintain it. Knowing how to monitor something is as important as getting it started. We take our cars in for a periodic tune-up. Why not do the same for our money?

Your financial life is personal to you; that's why it's called personal finance. There are no one-size-fits-all answers. There are the solutions that work just for you.

I'm on a mission to help people change the way they think about money. I've been in the financial services world for over 35 years, in a variety of roles, including insurance agent, fee-based insurance consultant working with clients and financial planners, litigation consultant, and member of the California Department of Insurance Curriculum Board, as well as an author and writer.

Over the years, even when working with the most knowledgeable advisors, the most common insurance question was, "Is this policy any good, and what should my client do?" While there were technical questions that needed to be addressed, there was always that basic two-part question that formed the core.

Most people did not understand what they were buying, they had no idea how to monitor it, and their products often had nothing to do with their goals. They did not have healthy money habits. When working as an expert, I started with values, expectations, and communication while specializing in best practices and ethics. If every member of the financial services community followed a consumer-focused code of ethics, it would be a vastly different industry. However, that's not happening anytime soon.

I am focused on helping people take charge so they know what they are looking for, what questions to ask, where to get more information, and how everything fits together. I believe that we can all take control of our financial lives, in our own way. We all know that we need to save more than we spend; however, achieving that goal is like trying to diet. We all know when we need to lose weight, but diets usually don't work over the long term. What does work with money and dieting is changing how we think about it and creating healthy habits.

My adage is that if you give someone a fish, you feed them for a day. If you teach someone how to fish, you feed them for a lifetime. This planner will help you to a lifetime of financial preparedness and peace of mind through healthy money habits.

Find useful forms and information in the Get Ready Toolkit, available at www.tonysteuer.com.

The Get Ready Method

The Get Ready Method puts you in control of your financial life.

- **The big picture:** The Get Ready Method is an easy-to-use roadmap to help you understand how everything fits together.
- **Why it matters:** The financial world can be overwhelming, and it can be hard to know where to start. The Get Ready Method provides clarity to evaluate whether financial products meet your goals.
- **What is it?** The Get Ready Method is based on eight habits that will empower you with your money and transform your life. It includes an innovative and unique financial calendar system with a weekly action item to help you keep all areas of your financial life up to date and on track.

This planner walks you through all areas of your financial life. We'll begin by building useful habits, then put them to use in planning, calculating, and reviewing key financial information.

THE GET READY HABITS

Prepare for the year with the Get Ready Habits.

Habit 1: Goals defined

"The only limit to the height of your achievements is the reach of your dreams and your willingness to work for them."

—MICHELLE OBAMA

- Your goals should be realistic, specific, and important to you.
- Be goal oriented, rather than product oriented.
- Consider a concrete time horizon for your goals: How long do you have?
- Prioritize your goals.

Ask yourself:

- What is important to you? What does financial success mean to you?
- What does your dream life look like?
- What do you want to achieve?

Habit 2: Educate yourself

"Learning is not attained by chance; it must be sought for with ardor and diligence."
—ABIGAIL ADAMS

- Learn what you need to know to make an informed decision.
- Your source of information should be qualified and unbiased.
- Understand how to use your knowledge.
- If you don't understand something, walk away.
- Keep information fresh.

Ask yourself:

- Do you have the information to make informed decisions?
- Do you know where to access qualified and unbiased information?
- What resources are available?
- Do you feel comfortable implementing your knowledge?
- How do you react to something you don't understand? Are you open to admitting it, or do you forge ahead?
- Are you comfortable walking away, even if that seems uncomfortable?
- Do you keep your information fresh or rely on old information?

Habit 3: Think about how you think

"A strong, positive self-image is the best possible preparation for success."
—JOYCE BROTHERS

- Understand how you think.
- Have a positive money mindset.
- Be judgment-free.
- Review your habits and processes.
- Act with intent.

Ask yourself:

- How do you feel about money?
- Are you stressed by money?
- Do you have a positive and healthy mindset about money?
- Is there anything that's giving you a negative money mindset?
- Are you judgment-free when it comes to your money? Or are you hard on yourself?
- What money habits do you feel are working?
- What money habits would you like to improve?
- Do you act with intent when it comes to your money? Or do you make impetuous decisions?
- Do you feel comfortable talking about money? Have you talked with your family about money?

Habit 4: Relevancy to you

"Always remember that you are absolutely unique. Just like everyone else."
—MARGARET MEAD

- Know your money story.
- Align with your values.
- Have your own definition of success.
- Customize products to fit your needs; you are unique, and there is no one-size-fits-all.
- Understand your money story so you know what you need to work on.

Ask yourself:

- What's your personal money story? Do you have a positive or negative history with money?
- What's your personal definition of success when it comes to money?
- What are your values when it comes to money?
- Do you consider your values when making money decisions? Do you align your decisions with your values?
- Do you think about your goals and what's right for you when thinking about a financial product? Or do you think about the product first?
- Do you tend to do what everyone else is doing, or do you stay true to your path?

Habit 5: Evaluate your options

"Whenever you're making an important decision, first ask if it gets you closer to your goals or farther away. If the answer is closer, pull the trigger. If it's farther away, make a different choice. Conscious choice making is a critical step in making your dreams a reality."
—JILLIAN MICHAELS

- Always evaluate your options.
- Monitor your expenses.
- Be wary of hidden costs and expenses.
- Consider the true (total) cost of a purchase.
- You have the right to choose.

Ask yourself:

- Do you evaluate all of your options, or do you tend to only look at one?
- How well do you feel you're monitoring your expenses?
- Do you feel like you understand the costs and expenses when it comes to money?
- Do you concentrate on return rather than expenses? If you reduce your expenses by 1 percent, that will increase your return by 1 percent.
- Do you think about the true (total) cost when you make a purchase such as a car? The true cost includes the price of the car, car insurance, loan interest, registration, and maintenance.
- Do you feel like you have the right to choose, or do you feel persuaded to purchase a product?

Habit 6: Assemble the pieces

"With organization comes empowerment."

—Lynda Peterson

- Know your resources.
- Gather all of your financial information.
- Consider how everything fits together.
- Determine whether you are missing anything.
- Terminate anything that is no longer needed.

Ask yourself:

- Do you have an overview of all of your resources? In other words, do you take an overall view of your financial life, or do you look at each product separately?
- Is all of your financial information available in one place, such as a spreadsheet or app?
- Do you understand how everything fits together?
- Are you able to tell if anything is missing?
- Do you terminate financial products and services that you no longer need, or do you tend to let them continue in the background?

Habit 7: Detailed focus

"It's important to pay attention to detail and win the small battles."

—Cara Hendry

- Take time to review details.
- Details lead to success.
- Have reasonable expectations.
- Seek balance in your financial life.
- Know when you need professional advice.

Ask yourself:

- How do you feel about details?
- Do you take the time to review details? Small details can make a significant difference.
- Do you feel like learning more about the details would lead to greater financial success?
- Do you have reasonable expectations? Or do you tend to overstate your expectations?
- Do you seek balance in your financial life?
- Do you seek out a professional advisor when you need help? Are you comfortable working with an advisor?

Habit 8: Yearly review

"Review is essential to evaluation, which is essential to progress."

—MELISSA STEGINUS

- Follow the Get Ready 52-Week Financial Calendar.
- Keep everything up to date.
- Life events require changes.
- Products and services change.
- Ensure that nothing falls through the cracks.

Ask yourself:

- What's your current method for reviewing your financial life?
- How do you feel about being guided by the Get Ready Financial Calendar?
- Do you feel like you keep everything up to date? Is this important to you?
- Do you update your financial products and services when you have a life event?
- Do you have a system to help ensure that nothing falls through the cracks?

VISION BOARD

Next, you'll create a vision board. Think about the most important things to your financial future. These can be the goals from Get Ready Habit 1 or loftier dreams for down the road. You can write down notes, paste some pictures, create a mind map, or add whatever helps you visualize your goals.

FIXED DATES

There are several fixed dates that will be important to the year ahead. Familiarize yourself with them and jot these down in your calendar.

FIXED AGES

Certain financial events occur when you hit a specific age. Will you hit any of these important thresholds this year? If so, add it to your calendar.

MONTHLY FOCUS AREA

Each month, we'll focus on one crucial area of your financial life. This focus will set you up for success in the weekly activities that follow.

WEEKLY ACTION ITEMS

Each week, you'll have a goal to accomplish. Keep track of your progress with the Get Ready Habits (and any of your own).

MONTHLY REFLECTION

At the end of each month, you'll be able to reflect on the month. You can check your progress toward your goals and make any adjustments you'll need to stay on track.

QUARTERLY REFLECTIONS

Every three months, you'll have the opportunity to reflect on the Get Ready Habits.

YEAR-END SUMMARY

At the end of the year, we'll have a summary that you can have as an easy reference for yourself, your family members, and your advisors and coaches.

JOIN THE GET READY MOVEMENT

GET READY. STAY PREPARED. Take control of your finances and feel empowered around your money. Change the way you think about money with a proven, easy-to-use, nonjudgmental system.

START YOUR OWN GET READY FINANCIAL PREPAREDNESS CLUB

Join up with friends and family to prepare for your financial future together and hold each other accountable.

TAKEAWAYS

The Get Ready Method provides a framework that

- is easy to use,
- fits who you are,
- reflects your values,
- creates a healthy mindset,
- helps you gain clarity,
- helps you create healthy money habits,
- empowers you,
- can be used for any financial product or service,
- assesses how your products and services are working,
- helps you create a plan,
- can be used with others including family members and advisors, and
- helps you stay on track.

THE BOTTOM LINE

The Get Ready Method will empower and educate you so you can be prepared, take control, and transform your financial life.

Vision Board

Fixed Dates to Add to Your Calendar

Add these dates to your planner and to your calendar. When tax deadlines fall on a Saturday, Sunday, or a holiday, the deadline is the next business day. Subscribe to the Get Ready Newsletter to receive reminders of these dates.

January

- January 15: Fourth-quarter estimated tax payment due for self-employed or other fourth-quarter income that requires quarterly estimated taxes.
- January 15: Individual health care coverage open enrollment ends for the Federal Health Care Insurance Exchange at www.healthcare.gov. States with their own health care exchange will have open enrollment typically starting on November 1 of the prior year and will usually have longer open-enrollment periods. You can find links to your state's health insurance marketplace at www .healthcare.gov/marketplace-in-your-state.
- January 31: Form W-2s (for employees), Form 1099-NECs (for self-employed, formerly reported on Form 1099-Misc), Form 1099-Misc (miscellaneous income), and Form 1098-T (loan interest) should start to arrive in the mail. These are required to be sent out by January 31, so they should also be available online today if the payer offers that option.
- January 31: Tax-filing (optionally) due if you didn't pay your last installment of estimated tax by January 17. You may choose (but aren't required) to file your income tax return (Form 1040 or Form 1040-SR) by January 31. Filing your return and paying all taxes by January 31 prevents any penalty for late payment of the last installment.
- Late January: Federal tax filing with the IRS starts.
- Late January: Social Security cost-of-living adjustments go into effect.
- Late January: There are generally a series of changes to the premiums, deductibles, and coinsurance for the four Medicare plans (part A, B, C, or D).
- Late January: Changes to retirement savings rules take effect. Contribution limits may increase each year.

February

- Watch for corrected tax forms. A corrected form replaces any prior form.
- Certain mutual funds could restate their distribution information after your initial Form 1099 is mailed to you at the end of January. Though not common, when such fixes are necessary, a corrected 1099 is usually mailed sometime in February.

March

- March 15: Maximum extension deadline for flexible spending account (FSA) claims.

April

- April 1: Individual retirement accounts (IRAs) and 401(k)s have a required minimum distribution due by April 1 if you turn age 73 during the calendar year. If you miss the deadline, you may be assessed with a penalty.
- April 15: File federal and state income tax returns. Request an extension if necessary. States have different rules, so check with your state tax authority. Fines and penalties can be assessed for missing deadlines. If you want an automatic six-month extension to file the return, file Form 4868 and pay what you estimate you owe in tax to avoid penalties and interest.
- April 15: First-quarter estimated tax payment due if you are self-employed or have other first-quarter income that requires you to pay quarterly estimated taxes.
- April 15: The last day you can contribute to an IRA for the prior calendar year.
- April 15: The last day that you can contribute to a health savings account (HSA) for the prior calendar year.
- April 15: The due date for self-employers to contribute to a solo 401(k) or an SEP for the prior calendar year.
- April 15: The deadline to withdraw excess IRA contributions made in the prior calendar year.

May

- None

June

- June 15: Second-quarter estimated tax payment due if you are self-employed or have other second-quarter income that requires you to pay quarterly estimated taxes.
- June 15: Deadline to file IRS Form 1040 or Form 1040-SR and pay any tax, interest, and penalties if you are a US resident living outside the United States and Puerto Rico. File Form 4868 to obtain four additional months (until October 15) to file and pay what you estimate you owe in tax to avoid penalties and interest. Then, file Form 1040 or Form 1040-SR by October 15.
- June 15: Tax return due for military personnel who are serving or living outside the US. If you want a four-month filing extension, you must apply by this date. If you're in a combat zone, you may be able to further extend the filing deadline.
- June 30: Federal deadline to file the Free Application for Federal Student Aid (FAFSA) online. However, states and colleges may ask for the FAFSA sooner, so check to see the deadline where you're applying.

July

- None

August

- None

September

- September 15: Third-quarter estimated tax payment due if you are self-employed or have other third-quarter income that requires you to pay quarterly estimated taxes.

October

- October 1: Final day to establish a SIMPLE IRA this year for your small business.
- October 1: First chance to apply for federal student aid for the following year. It's best to complete the FAFSA as early as possible because states and colleges use it to award their own grants, scholarships, and loans, and that aid is limited.
- October 15: Extended filing deadline for most small businesses and last day to open an individual 401(k) or SEP IRA for this year.
- October 15: Medicare open enrollment starts. Learn more at www.medicare.gov.
- October 15: Extended individual tax returns due. If you had an automatic six-month extension to file your return for this year, file Form 1040 or Form 1040-SR and pay any tax, interest, and penalties due.
- Employers may start open enrollment for employee benefits. Check with your employer to confirm the open enrollment start and end dates.

November

- November 1: Open enrollment starts for the Federal Health Care Insurance Exchange. State health care exchanges will also typically start their open enrollment. Learn more and find links to state exchanges at www.healthcare.gov.
- Employers may start open enrollment for employee benefits. Open enrollment usually also closes in November. Check with your employer to confirm the open enrollment start and end dates.

December

- December 7: Medicare open enrollment ends. Learn more at www.medicare.gov.
- December 15: Individual health care coverage open enrollment ends for the Federal Health Care Insurance Exchange. States that maintain their own health care exchange will usually have longer open enrollment periods. Learn more and find links to your state's health care exchange at www.healthcare.gov.
- December 31: Flexible spending account (FSA) and dependent care spending account (DCSA) claim deadlines. Employers can extend the claim deadline for FSAs to March 15 of the following year. Your employer may allow you to carry over $500 in unused funds to the following year; if they do not, this is the "use it or lose it" date. Health savings accounts (HSAs) allow you to carry over your full balance.
- December 31: Complete any charitable donations.
- December 31: Contributions to employer-sponsored retirement plans (401(k), 403(b), 457, or federal thrift savings) must be completed.
- December 31: If you had to take your first required minimum distribution (RMD) from your IRA or 401(k) by April 1, you must take your second RMD by December 31.

Fixed Ages

If you will hit any of these age-related milestones this year, be sure to add them to the appropriate monthly calendar.

- Birth: Can be named as beneficiary of 529 plan account and owner of Uniform Trust to Minors Act (UTMA)/Uniform Gift to Minors Act (UGMA) accounts.
- 13: Child no longer eligible for child and dependent care credit.
- 17: Child no longer eligible for Child Tax Credit.
- 18: Age of majority in most states.
- 18: Age of termination for some UGMA and UTMA accounts.
- 18: Child no longer subject to Kiddie Tax (unless full-time student).
- 18: Can sign legally binding contracts and get a credit card. Parents need permission for health information.
- 19: Can no longer be claimed as a qualifying child dependent if not in college.
- 21: Can start contributing to a SEP IRA.
- 21: Age of majority in some states.
- 21: Age of termination for some UGMA and UTMA accounts.
- 24: Child who is a full-time student no longer subject to Kiddie Tax.
- 24: Can no longer be claimed as a qualifying child dependent if in college.
- 26: Can no longer be on parents' health insurance.
- 50: Can begin making catch-up contributions, an extra amount that those over age 50 can add to their 401(k) and other retirement accounts.
- 50: Eligible for Social Security benefits as a disabled widow or widower.
- 55: Eligible to make catch-up contributions to an HSA.
- 55: Eligible for penalty exceptions for certain withdrawals from retirement accounts.
- 59 + 6 months: No more tax penalties on early withdrawals from employer-provided retirement savings plans such as 401(k)s and IRAs.
- 60: Eligible to claim Social Security survivor benefits as a widow or widower (early, at a reduced rate).
- 62: Earliest age to collect Social Security benefits. If you claim benefits earlier than your full retirement age, you will receive a lower monthly benefit.
- 62: Eligible to qualify for a reverse mortgage.
- 64 + 9 months: Three months before your 65th birthday, you can apply for Medicare. This is the age when you sign up for Medicare Parts A, B, and D; Medicare Supplements; or Medicare Advantage. This must be done within six months of turning 65.
- 65: Eligible for nonmedical withdrawals from HSA without a penalty.
- 65, 66, and 67: Full retirement age, depending on when you were born. You can earn Social Security delayed retirement credits, which will increase your monthly benefit for each month that claiming is delayed between your full retirement age and age 70.
- 66: Full retirement age if born between 1943–1954.
- 66 + 2 months: Full retirement age if born in 1955.
- 66 + 4 months: Full retirement age if born in 1956.
- 66 + 6 months: Full retirement age if born in 1957.
- 66 + 8 months: Full retirement age if born in 1958.
- 66 + 10 months: Full retirement age if born in 1959.
- 67: Full retirement age if born in 1960 or later.
- 70: Maximum Social Security benefit is reached. Social Security benefits must be taken if claiming has been delayed.
- 70 + 6 months: Eligible to make a qualified charitable distribution.
- 73: Required minimum distribution age if born before 1960. You're now subject to required minimum distributions from your traditional retirement accounts. Roth accounts and HSAs don't have required minimum distributions.
- 75: Required minimum distribution age if born in 1960 or later. You're now subject to required minimum distributions from your traditional retirement accounts.

Habits and Planning

MONTH 1

	Sunday	Monday	Tuesday	Wednesday	Thursday	Friday	Saturday
Week 1							
Week 2							
Week 3							
Week 4							

The big picture: Plan for the year with healthy habits.

Why it's important: Positive change comes from healthy habits. Planning for the year ahead will help you be prepared.

Here's what works: This month we'll focus on these activities:

- Review the Get Ready Method. Implement the Get Ready Habits and follow the Get Ready Financial Calendar.
- Define your goals and priorities. This will give you a clear mission for your financial journey.
- Plan for life stages. As we go through life, our needs and goals will evolve.
- Forecast life events. Life events bring new opportunities that require updating relevant financial products and services.

ON THE CALENDAR

On the monthly calendar, write in the following items:

- The month and days
- Any fixed dates
- When you're expecting income
- Any bills due this month—mark the payment date seven days prior to the due date, along with the due date
- Life events
- Items from your to-do list

To-do list:

- Action steps to take this month
- Adjustments to make
- People to talk to
- Ways to make this month great
- Things you are looking forward to this month
- Distractions to avoid

- _____
- _____

Wheel segments: Yearly Review, Goals Defined, Educate Yourself, Think About How You Think, Relevancy To You, Evaluate Your Options, Assemble the Pieces, Detailed Focus

THE BOTTOM LINE

Having a plan and developing beneficial habits will help you meet your goals and keep everything up to date.

Review the Get Ready Habits

Sunday:

Monday:

Tuesday:

Wednesday:

Thursday:

Friday:

Saturday:

The big picture: The Get Ready Method puts you in control of your financial life.

Why it matters: The financial world can be overwhelming, and it can be hard to know where to start. The Get Ready Method helps you gain healthy habits and review all of the areas of your financial life.

What are your three big goals for the week?

· Get Ready Goal: Review the Get Ready Habits.

· Goal 1: _____

· Goal 2: _____

Here's what works: Review the Get Ready Habits.

· Goals defined: What are they, are they important, and what is their time period?

· Educate yourself: Know how to use what you learn and keep it fresh.

· Think about how you think: Have a positive mindset and act with intent.

· Relevancy to you: Understand who you are and align with your values.

· Evaluate your options: Choose wisely and monitor fees and expenses.

· Assemble the pieces: Know how everything fits together and what's missing.

· Detailed focus: Review the details, seek balance, and know when you need help.

· Yearly review: Keep up to date and follow the Get Ready Method.

The Get Ready Method provides an easy-to-use roadmap to help you understand how everything fits together with a weekly action item to help you stay on track and keep all areas of your financial life up to date.

To-do list:

- Determine any changes in your life that may impact your goals.
- Determine what adjustments you need to make.
- Determine which advisors you will discuss this with.

- _____

- _____

Positive Habit Maker							
Habit	S	M	T	W	T	F	S
Goals defined							
Educate yourself							
Think about how you think							
Relevancy to you							
Evaluate your options							
Assemble the pieces							
Detailed focus							
Yearly review							

THE BOTTOM LINE

The Get Ready Habits will empower you to take control of your financial life.

Define Your Goals and Priorities

Sunday:
Monday:
Tuesday:
Wednesday:
Thursday:
Friday:
Saturday:

The big picture: Financial success requires thinking about your goals first.

Why it matters: We often think about the financial product first. We need to consider what we want to accomplish and then see what product will help us achieve our goals. Defining your goals helps you stay focused and on track.

What are your goals this week?

- Get Ready Goal: Define your goals and priorities.
- Goal 1: _____
- Goal 2: _____

Here's what works: Set your goals with the SMART principles and consider priority.

- **Specific:** What do you want to accomplish? Being specific makes the goal achievable.
- **Measurable:** How much do you need? This allows you to easily determine if you are meeting your goal.
- **Achievable:** How can you accomplish this goal? This defines if the goal is realistic.
- **Relevant:** Can you (and will you) meet this goal? Relevance makes sure that the goal really matters to you and aligns with the rest of your financial life.
- **Time-bound:** When do you need to complete this goal? Having a target date gives you a deadline to focus on.
- Priority: How important is this goal? Assigning priority helps you decide which goals to focus on.

In the table below, enter your three big goals for the year and apply the SMART principles and priority. You'll also be able to set goals for each quarter, month, and week.

SMART + priority	Example	Goal 1	Goal 2	Goal 3
Specific	Create a rainy day fund.			
Measurable	$5,000	$	$	$
Achievable	$208 a month/$104 a paycheck	$	$	$
Realistic	Yes, auto-transfer $104 per paycheck to rainy day fund	$	$	$
Time-bound	In 24 months			
Priority	High priority			
Notes				

To-do list:

· Add your goals to the year-end summary (see week 52).

· List any changes in your life that may impact your goals.

· Make any adjustments you need.

· List the advisors you will discuss this with.

· _____

· _____

Positive Habit Maker							
Habit	S	M	T	W	T	F	S
Goals defined							
Educate yourself							
Think about how you think							
Relevancy to you							
Evaluate your options							
Assemble the pieces							
Detailed focus							
Yearly review							

THE BOTTOM LINE

Setting goals and priorities will give you a clear mission for your financial journey.

Plan for Life Stages

Sunday:

Monday:

Tuesday:

Wednesday:

Thursday:

Friday:

Saturday:

The big picture: Our financial needs change as we go through the stages of life.

Why it matters: Understanding how our financial needs change throughout our lives allows us to stay on track and meet our goals.

Your life stage will impact your financial journey. Here are the four main life stages with a few things to focus on:

STARTING OUT

From the moment that you earn your first dollar, you are on your financial journey. For most of us, this takes place when we enter the workforce, whether that's at age 18 or after graduating from college. At this stage, you'll want to think about these actions:

· Setting goals
· Starting to save for financial independence
· Making sure you're protecting yourself with insurance, including your income and home (renters insurance)
· Creating a rainy day fund
· Establishing credit history
· Participating in employee benefit plans for insurance and retirement
· Paying back any student loans

ACCUMULATION

During your peak income years, you are building your career or starting your own business. Focus on these actions:

· Meeting goals, including your financial independence

- Managing and growing wealth by following an Investment Policy Statement
- Protecting your income with disability insurance and your family with life insurance
- Saving for your kids, including a 529 plan for college
- Creating your estate plan
- Managing debt and avoiding lifestyle creep

FINANCIAL INDEPENDENCE

When you retire (or semi-retire) from the workforce and are no longer dependent on earned income, you have reached financial independence. At this stage, focus on these actions:

- Optimizing your financial independence paycheck
- Updating your Investment Policy Statement from accumulation to distribution
- Moving away from employer-paid health insurance; considering long-term care insurance
- Updating your will and estate plan

GOLDEN YEARS

You're in your 70s, 80s, or 90s and ready to reap the rewards you've built over your lifetime. Now, you should focus on these actions:

- Estate planning and charitable bequests to ensure your legacy
- Creating health and caregiving plans and powers of attorney
- Funding college savings accounts for and making gifts to your grandchildren and beyond

Here's what works: In the table below, add any life stage coming up this year and what focus areas will need attention. Then you can add an item to the corresponding week's to-do list. What's your plan for each focus area? You can come back to this during the year and update as needed.

Focus area	Life stage
Habits and planning	
Be prepared	
Your team	
Cash flow	
Net worth	
Strategy review	
Are you protected?	
Your legacy	
Financial independence	
Find value	
Monitor your personal information	
Wrap up loose ends	
Notes	

What are your three big goals for this week?

- Get Ready Goal: Plan for life stages.
- Goal 1: _____
- Goal 2: _____
- Goal 3: _____

To-do list:

- Add your life stage to the year-end summary (see week 52).
- If you are entering a new life stage, add it to your calendar.
- List any adjustments you need to make.
- List the advisors you will discuss this with.
- _____
- _____

Positive Habit Maker							
Habit	S	M	T	W	T	F	S
Goals defined							
Educate yourself							
Think about how you think							
Relevancy to you							
Evaluate your options							
Assemble the pieces							
Detailed focus							
Yearly review							

THE BOTTOM LINE

As you go through life, review all areas to make sure you stay on track to meet your goals.

Plan for Upcoming Life Events

The big picture: Life events can impact different areas of our financial life.

Why it matters: Every life event will impact our goals and how we can achieve them. Following the Get Ready Method helps you know what to update and what to consider.

What are your three big goals this week?

- Get Ready Goal: Plan for upcoming life events.
- Goal 1: _____
- Goal 2: _____

Here's what works: Life events will impact different areas of your financial life. What follows is a starting point for some things to think about.

- **Business ownership:** Insurance for the business. Manage debt. Health insurance. Retirement plan. Disability insurance.
- **Caregiving:** Family meeting (communicate wishes). Update estate plan. Have power of attorney (POA). Health care plan. Health care team. Budget for caregiving—what insurance, assets? Monitor finances (watch for fraud).
- **Disability:** File for claims. Continue saving for goals. Update cash flow.
- **Disaster recovery:** Use your rainy day fund if needed. File insurance claims. If possible, avoid taking on debt or consider options for debt (disaster loans and claims).
- **Divorce:** Estate planning update. Update beneficiaries. Document update if name change. Property titles. Qualified Domestic Relations Order (QDRO) for splitting a retirement plan or pension. Close joint bank accounts, credit cards, loans, and other accounts. Update investment strategy.

Sunday:

Monday:

Tuesday:

Wednesday:

Thursday:

Friday:

Saturday:

- **Financial independence and retirement:** Design financial independence paycheck. Obtain individual health insurance or Medicare. Terminate disability insurance. Modify or terminate life insurance. Plan for longevity.
- **Home purchase:** Consider true cost of buying home including property taxes, homeowners insurance, maintenance costs, etc.
- **Inheritance and windfalls:** Consult a financial advisor. Make a plan before spending any money. Manage cash flow. A high percentage of people blow through their windfall.
- **Leaving a job:** Get individual insurance to replace any you will lose—if not starting a new job. Decide on what to do with employer-provided retirement plan. Use up your FSA and any paid time off (PTO/sick days/vacation days). 401(k) plan (rollover to IRA or new employer 401(k) or maintain?). Review vesting schedules for retirement plan contributions and stock plans. Estimate tax liabilities.
- **Marriage and domestic partnership:** Family meeting. Decide on separate or shared finances, tax filing status, insurance (set separate and joint goals). Estate planning update. Document update if name change. Update beneficiaries. Property titles. Update investment strategy.
- **Military:** Understand military insurance, retirement, and other benefits. Estate planning.
- **Moving:** Update all financial account records. Review homeowners and auto insurance as location will impact premium amounts.
- **Parenthood (birth, adoption, foster):** Life insurance. College savings account. Estate planning update. Update beneficiaries. Update health insurance. Plan for child-related costs. Research parental leave. Apply for a social security number (so you can claim your new dependent).
- **Pet ownership:** Pet insurance. Pet estate planning—pet guardian physical and financial.
- **Special-needs child:** Estate planning will with guardian. Special needs trust. ABLE (Achieving a Better Life Experience) account. Government benefits.
- **Starting a job:** Negotiate salary—get paid what you're worth (research gender pay gap). Maximize employee benefit usage. Participate in 401(k) and make sure to get match. Review health insurance.
- **Starting out (turning 18) and college years:** Rainy day fund. Cash flow plan. Manage debt. Build credit score. Savings plan. Start investing (create an investment strategy). Health insurance. Auto insurance (you'll need to get your own). Renters insurance. Health care POA for parents. Manage debt and student loans (apply for financial aid/FAFSA) if going to college. Work. Set goals.
- **Widowhood:** Get certified copies of death certificate. Settle the estate. Execute will and trust. File insurance claims. Notify Social Security. Claim benefits through deceased's employee benefits. Notify financial providers, credit bureaus, utilities, and so on. Update estate plan and beneficiary designations. Remove deceased from accounts. Property titles. Update investment strategy.

In the table below, add any life events coming up this year and what focus areas will need attention. Then you can add an item to the corresponding week's to-do list. What's your plan for each focus area? You can come back to this during the year and update as needed.

Focus area	Life Event	Life Event
Habits and planning		
Be prepared		
Your team		
Cash flow		
Net worth		
Strategy review		
Are you protected?		
Your legacy		
Financial independence		
Find value		
Monitor your personal information		
Wrap up loose ends		
Notes		

To-do list:

- Add your life events to the year-end summary (see week 52).
- List any life events that have recently passed or are coming up.
- Write down your plan for any recent or upcoming life events.
- List the advisors you will discuss this with.

- _____

- _____

Positive Habit Maker							
Habit	S	M	T	W	T	F	S
Goals defined							
Educate yourself							
Think about how you think							
Relevancy to you							
Evaluate your options							
Assemble the pieces							
Detailed focus							
Yearly review							

THE BOTTOM LINE

Stay prepared by updating your financial life as you encounter life events.

Monthly Reflection

What were your five biggest wins?

1.

2.

3.

4.

5.

ASK YOURSELF:

- How did the month go for you?
- What goals did you meet this month?
- What challenges did you overcome?
- How is your progress with the Get Ready Habits?
- How did you do with your habits?

- What were your biggest lessons learned?
- What were your insights this month?
- What tasks do you still need to work on?
- How will you improve next month?
- How will you celebrate your wins this month?

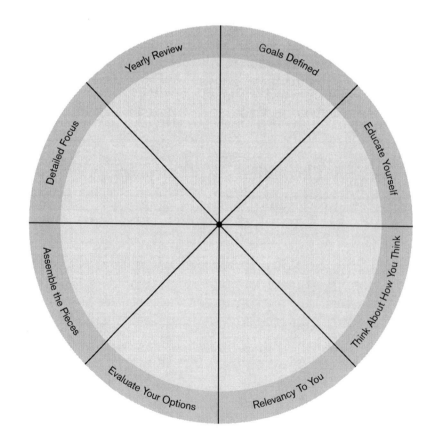

Expense Tracker

Date	Payee	Category/Purpose	Amount

Be Prepared

MONTH 2

	Sunday	Monday	Tuesday	Wednesday	Thursday	Friday	Saturday
Week 5							
Week 6							
Week 7							
Week 8							

The big picture: Being prepared is key to navigating life events.

Why it's important: Taking the time to prepare will help you be ready for anything. It's important to stay prepared as your life changes.

Here's what works: This month we'll focus on these action items:

- Organizing your financial documents. Organizing your financial life will make your life easier.
- Decluttering your documents. Knowing what to keep and what you can toss is essential.
- Updating your home inventory. This can help you when filing an insurance claim.
- Creating a critical emergency action list. Know what you need to do in the event of an emergency, including location of essential financial documents.

ON THE CALENDAR

On the monthly calendar, write in the following items:

- The month and days
- Any fixed dates
- When you're expecting income
- Any bills due this month—mark the payment date seven days prior to the due date, along with the due date
- Life events
- Items from your to-do list

 **To-do list:**

- Action steps to take this month
- Adjustments to make
- People to talk to
- Ways to make this month great
- Things you are looking forward to this month
- Distractions to avoid

- _____
- _____

THE BOTTOM LINE

Be prepared so you can be ready for anything.

Organize Your Financial Documents

Sunday:
Monday:
Tuesday:
Wednesday:
Thursday:
Friday:
Saturday:

The big picture: Organizing your financial life will make your life easier. You'll be able to reduce stress and find the information you need.

Why it matters: Getting organized will help you be able to find the information you need, when you need it.

· Your financial life is dynamic and always changing.
· Being able to quickly find your important documents will help your spouse, children, or executor in the event you become incapacitated or pass away.
· It will also help you during your life—when you apply for a loan, meet with your estate planning attorney, or are forced to leave your house in an emergency.

What are your three big goals this week?

· Get Ready Goal: Organize your financial documents.
· Goal 1: _____
· Goal 2: _____

Here's what works: Enter in the table below where your current documents are located.

· For physical documents, you'll need a binder with tabbed dividers for each of the sections below. On your computer, set up a folder called "Financial First Aid Kit" and then subfolders for each of the sections.

I also encourage you to back them up and keep them secure in one or more of the following places: a fireproof safe; a safe-deposit box; your cloud storage account, like Apple iCloud or Dropbox, for digital storage; and a USB thumb drive for digital storage, which you can then keep safe in your personal financial binder.

Document type	Where are these documents?	Notes
Personal papers and documents		
Assets		
Retirement plans		
Home and real property		
Income		
Debts, loans, expenses, and taxes		
Insurance		
Estate planning		
Identity monitoring		

To-do list:

- Add the location of your documents to the year-end summary (see week 52).
- List any changes that may impact how you organize your documents.
- List any adjustments to your current organizational system to improve it.
- _____
- _____

Positive Habit Maker							
Habit	S	M	T	W	T	F	S
Goals defined							
Educate yourself							
Think about how you think							
Relevancy to you							
Evaluate your options							
Assemble the pieces							
Detailed focus							
Yearly review							

THE BOTTOM LINE

Commit yourself to becoming financially organized. Set this as a priority.

Declutter Your Documents

Sunday:	
Monday:	
Tuesday:	
Wednesday:	
Thursday:	
Friday:	
Saturday:	

The big picture: While it's important to cut down on the clutter, you need to know what's essential and what you can get rid of.

Why it matters: Knowing what documents to keep will guide you in making sure that you have the documents that you need, as well as knowing what documents you can safely get rid of.

What are your three big goals this week?

· Get Ready Goal: Declutter your documents.

· Goal 1: _____

· Goal 2: _____

Here's what works: In the table below, you can add the location and decluttering status.

· If there is no purge date, you'll probably want to keep that document forever or use your best judgment on how long to keep it.

· All purged documents should be shredded to help prevent identity theft.

· Please note that these are just recommendations and are not legal or tax advice. You may wish to seek expert advice if you have concerns about purging a document.

Document type	Location	How long to keep	Decluttering status
Bank account records		Keep statements and canceled checks for six years (receipts until statement reconciliation).	
Car title, registration, repair records		Until six months after sale.	
Credit card statements		If used for tax purposes, keep for six years; otherwise, shred statements and receipts after reconciling statement, or longer if you wish to return something.	
Home purchase documents		Keep on hand for at least six years after sale of home.	
Insurance policies		Until coverage ends or is canceled.	
Pay stubs		Keep for six years.	
Rental agreements		Retain for up to six years after agreement is terminated.	
Student loan records		Keep indefinitely as proof of payoff.	

One more thing: I keep items in files for seven years for any closed account with all of my tax documentations, and after seven years, I destroy the physical documents. For other documents, if there is no recommended purge date, I will usually keep them forever. With the ability to scan documents, I keep digital copies forever on my computer.

To-do list:

- List any changes to your life that may impact how you declutter your documents.
- List any adjustments you need to make.
- Review documents to purge with the appropriate advisor.

- _____

- _____

Positive Habit Maker							
Habit	S	M	T	W	T	F	S
Goals defined							
Educate yourself							
Think about how you think							
Relevancy to you							
Evaluate your options							
Assemble the pieces							
Detailed focus							
Yearly review							

THE BOTTOM LINE

Knowing what documents to keep and what you can purge will help you make sure you have the right documents when needed.

Update Your Home Inventory

The big picture: Updating your home inventory will help you be prepared when faced with financial adversity.

Why it matters: It's important to keep a record of your major personal property items in the event that you have to file an insurance claim in case of a burglary, fire, flood, earthquake, or other event.

- If you don't have a record, you won't be able to file an insurance claim, police report, or find a replacement.

What are your three big goals this week?

- Get Ready Goal: Update your home inventory.
- Goal 1: _____
- Goal 2: _____

Here's what works: In the table below, you can add the inventory status and notes for the most common locations in your residence (home, apartment, condo).

- Break it up and do one room at a time. No need to do your whole home in one day.
- Take photos of major property. Upload photos to a storage website such as iCloud or Dropbox.
- As you enter the current values for your property, estimate a price based on reasonable fair-market value. Be careful not to overvalue items such as appliances, computer equipment, car phones, and home entertainment items; these may not be worth as much as you think. A site such as eBay (www.ebay.com) will provide a good start for determining these values.
- Be sure to keep copies of receipts, purchase contracts, and appraisals. You'll need these if you file an insurance claim or something needs to be repaired.

Sunday:

Monday:

Tuesday:

Wednesday:

Thursday:

Friday:

Saturday:

Location	Inventory completed date	Notes
Living room		
Dining room		
Kitchen		
Bedroom 1		
Bedroom 2		
Bedroom 3		
Garage		
Other		
Other		

One more thing: Declutter your belongings for cash. As you do your inventory, set aside items that you can sell or donate.

 To-do list:

· Add the location of your home inventory to the year-end summary (see week 52).
· List any changes in your life that may impact your home inventory, such as a new home or apartment.
· List any adjustments you need to make.
· List any advisors you need to talk with.

· _____

· _____

Positive Habit Maker							
Habit	S	M	T	W	T	F	S
Goals defined							
Educate yourself							
Think about how you think							
Relevancy to you							
Evaluate your options							
Assemble the pieces							
Detailed focus							
Yearly review							

THE BOTTOM LINE

A detailed home inventory will help you be prepared in the event of a theft or disaster.

Create a Critical Emergency Action List

The big picture: Do you know the steps to take in the event of an emergency?

Why it matters: Knowing the steps when there's an emergency will help you know what tasks need to be accomplished so that you don't forget anything important.

- During an emergency, you may have limited time to gather what you need, you may lose access to the internet, or you may realize you're lacking certain supplies.

What are your three big goals this week?

- Get Ready Goal: Create a critical emergency action list.
- Goal 1: _____
- Goal 2: _____

Check-in: Do you have a critical emergency action list or emergency action plan?

Here's what works: Create and update the list of the steps you'll take from the list below. A one-size-fits-all action plan may not address all your family's needs. It's important to take the time to think through the steps that are essential to you and your family.

- Review your emergency plan with all members of your family.
- The documents that you will need in an emergency include those that can help you manage your financial life: your driver's license (or other identification), passports, medical information including medication details, and insurance policy summaries (company name and policy number).

Sunday:

Monday:

Tuesday:

Wednesday:

Thursday:

Friday:

Saturday:

- Choose a meeting location for your family in the event of an emergency. It's a good idea to set primary as well as secondary locations.
- Review your evacuation procedures.
- Know how to shut off the water, gas, and main electrical switch to your home.
- Establish a communication plan. Set up an out-of-area contact that you and other family members can relay information to. Determine whether you and your family will also use an online resource to communicate with one another. Make sure everyone knows and understands your communication plan.
- Make sure your fire extinguishers are accessible and know how to use them. Keep in mind that sometimes fire extinguishers need to be refreshed, so check these regularly.
- Monitor your smoke, carbon dioxide, and other alarms. Replace the batteries in these and test each of them. A good practice is to do this twice a year when the time changes (you can add this to the planner).
- Know what items you will want to take with you in the event of an evacuation.

One more thing: Keep a copy of your critical emergency action list in an easy-to-find location, such as on your refrigerator. Also, keep a copy in your emergency kit (if you have one). Consider giving a copy (or partial copy) to a trusted relative, friend, or neighbor.

 To-do list:

- Are there any changes in your life that may impact your critical emergency action list?
- List any adjustments you will be making.
- List any advisors you will talk to about this.

- _____

- _____

Positive Habit Maker							
Habit	S	M	T	W	T	F	S
Goals defined							
Educate yourself							
Think about how you think							
Relevancy to you							
Evaluate your options							
Assemble the pieces							
Detailed focus							
Yearly review							

THE BOTTOM LINE

Life is uncertain, and things happen quickly. A critical emergency action list provides you a framework.

Monthly Reflection

What were your five biggest wins?

1.

2.

3.

4.

5.

ASK YOURSELF:

· How did the month go for you?

· What goals did you meet this month?

· What challenges did you overcome?

· How is your progress with the Get Ready Habits?

· How did you do with your habits?

· What were your biggest lessons learned?

· What were your insights this month?

· What tasks do you still need to work on?

· How will you improve next month?

· How will you celebrate your wins this month?

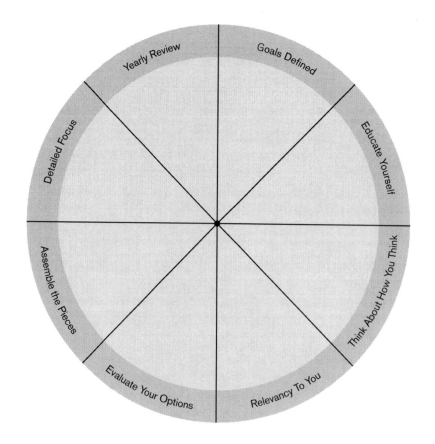

Expense Tracker

Date	Payee	Category/Purpose	Amount

Your Team

MONTH 3

	Sunday	Monday	Tuesday	Wednesday	Thursday	Friday	Saturday
Week 9							
Week 10							
Week 11							
Week 12							
Week 13							

The big picture: Check in with your team so everyone is on the same page.

Why it's important: Communicating with your family members ensures that everyone knows what each other's wishes are. Your advisors can help you make sure that everything is up to date and running efficiently.

Here's what works: This month, we'll focus on these action items:

- Have a family financial meeting. Check in with your partner and kids about the family finances. You can also check in with an accountability partner.
- Have a family transition meeting. Sit down and discuss plans and wishes with your parents and siblings.
- Review your advisory team. Make sure that you have the right advisors for your money.
- Review your support for the next generation. Review your strategy for providing financial support for your children, grandchildren, nieces, and nephews.

ON THE CALENDAR

On the monthly calendar, write in the following items:

- The month and days
- Any fixed dates
- When you're expecting income
- Any bills due this month—mark the payment date seven days prior to the due date, along with the due date
- Life events
- Items from your to-do list

 **To-do list:**

- Action steps to take this month
- Adjustments to make
- People to talk to
- Ways to make this month great
- Things you are looking forward to this month
- Distractions to avoid
- _____
- _____

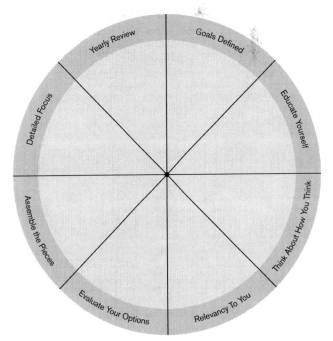

THE BOTTOM LINE

Communicating with members of your team will ensure that everyone is on the same page.

Have a Family Financial Meeting

Sunday:	
Monday:	
Tuesday:	
Wednesday:	
Thursday:	
Friday:	
Saturday:	

The big picture: An accountability meeting with your spouse, domestic partner, or other family members is a great way to review and communicate goals, priorities, and intentions with your immediate family.

Why it matters: Communicating with family members about finances keeps everyone on the same page. This includes your kids who will benefit from an early start with financial literacy.

· If you're single, consider meeting with an accountability partner. Having an accountability partner will help you stay on track and follow through.

What are your three big goals this week?

· Get Ready Goal: Have a family financial meeting.
· Goal 1: _____
· Goal 2: _____

Here's what works: Schedule your family financial meeting with a clear agenda and purpose so it will be productive. Because discussions about finances can be emotional, a meeting plan will allow everyone to more easily stick to the script.

· Each person in the family who works with or benefits from "house money" should be invited, including your kids. Involving kids can be a great way for them to learn and become financially literate.
· Guide the discussion during the meeting.
· Provide opportunities for everyone to talk. It's important that everyone in the family has a chance to communicate what their financial priorities, goals, and objectives are.
· Make sure to cover all the necessary topics. Are you focusing on maximizing retirement savings? Is your family saving for your children to go to college? Each objective that's relevant to your family's finances needs to be covered.

- Remember that you are striving to make a plan that works for all members of the family.
- Work together to set short-term, intermediate-term, and long-term financial goals.
- Designate financial family roles. This will help ensure the goals are accomplished and also provide everyone with a sense of ownership in the family's finances. Typically, one person handles the majority of financial tasks, such as paying bills and managing investments, but other family members can take on responsibilities as needed.
- Create a family transition plan. Plan for how other family members would take over in the event of an emergency.
- Share the family's financial information and any personal financial information with your spouse or domestic partner. Coordinate your financial lives so that you can each take over for the other person if needed. This can also help you reduce expenses by combining certain accounts, such as cellular and online services.
- Communicate where your financial documents and any information about your wishes are located.
- Make a plan in the event of your death. One way to take care of your family financially is to ensure they know what to do if you pass away.

To-do list:

- List any changes in your life that you need to cover.
- List any adjustments you need to make.

- _____

- _____

Positive Habit Maker							
Habit	S	M	T	W	T	F	S
Goals defined							
Educate yourself							
Think about how you think							
Relevancy to you							
Evaluate your options							
Assemble the pieces							
Detailed focus							
Yearly review							

THE BOTTOM LINE

Communication is key to managing your family finances.

Have a Family Transition Meeting with Parents and Siblings

Sunday:	
Monday:	
Tuesday:	
Wednesday:	
Thursday:	
Friday:	
Saturday:	

The big picture: Parents with adult children need to talk.
Why it matters: A family transition meeting will help ensure that there is a plan that can be followed to avoid issues later on.

- Your health care directives and final wishes can be followed. If no one knows about them, they can't be followed.
- Make sure that everyone knows how assets will be distributed.

What are your three big goals this week?

- Get Ready Goal: Have a family transition meeting with your parents and siblings.
- Goal 1: _____
- Goal 2: _____

Here's what works: Schedule the meeting.

- Be sure to review your health care wishes with your health care proxy. Provide your proxy with a copy of your health care directive.
- Review your final wishes with your family members. If you prefer not to review them, be sure to let them know the location of documents and instructions. Instructions and wishes can only be followed if they are known.
- Family members should know where you keep your financial documents.
- This will allow family members to be able to easily locate specific financial documents.
- If a family member has had changes in goals or priorities, discuss how this will impact your family's financial strategy.

- Discuss details on how you receive and pay your bills. This will allow a family member to step in to ensure that expenses are covered. Adult children can help aging parents manage their finances.
- Adult children can help protect their parents from becoming victims of financial predators if they are involved with their parents' finances. Providing limited access to financial accounts can help them watch for questionable transactions.
- Requesting duplicate statements, if appropriate, can also provide extra oversight. The client must sign off on this. The people receiving the statements don't have trading authority or capability; it is more for informational purposes.

One more thing: The key is that the parents need to be willing to open up about their financial life and understand that it is for everyone's benefit. This will help when it's time for an heir to step into their parents' financial life.

 To-do list:

- List any life changes that will impact your family transition plan.
- List any adjustments you need to make.
- List the advisors you will discuss this with.
- _____
- _____

Positive Habit Maker							
Habit	S	M	T	W	T	F	S
Goals defined							
Educate yourself							
Think about how you think							
Relevancy to you							
Evaluate your options							
Assemble the pieces							
Detailed focus							
Yearly review							

THE BOTTOM LINE

Open and ongoing communication helps make sure there is a smooth transition.

Review Your Advisory Team

Sunday:

Monday:

Tuesday:

Wednesday:

Thursday:

Friday:

Saturday:

The big picture: A qualified advisor can help guide you through complex matters.

Why it matters: Knowing when to call in someone with expertise is a key to success.

· Making the decision to hire an advisor depends on your comfort level and understanding of an issue, as well as the complexity of the issue.

What are your three big goals this week?

· Get Ready Goal: Review your advisory team.

· Goal 1: _____

· Goal 2: _____

Check-in: Review this list of the most common advisors to see if you have the right people on your team. You can log their contact information in the year-end summary in week 52.

· Accountants and tax professionals to help with your income taxes, tax planning, and other accounting issues
· An estate planning attorney to assist you with creating all of your estate planning documents, including wills, trusts, and powers of attorney
· Financial coaches to help in different areas of your financial life—be sure to check their qualifications and expertise
· Financial planners to help create your financial plan and manage the various components of a financial plan
· An insurance agent who specializes in the coverage you are looking for

Here's what works: Look for an advisor who has the right credentials and experience for the service or product that you're considering.

THE GET READY FINANCIAL STANDARDS

The Get Ready Financial Standards are reasonable expectations for you, as the consumer. Advisors and companies should adhere to these standards. Here are the Get Ready Financial Standards:

- Your advisor should act in your best interest.
- You should receive customized service appropriate to your needs.
- You have free choice.
- You should receive an answer to any question.
- You have the right to pay a fair price (or premium).
- You should always be informed.
- You should expect to be treated fairly and respectfully.
- You have the right to full disclosure and updates.
- You should receive quality service and fair resolutions (including claims handling).
- You should be able to change or cancel a financial service and be notified of any changes.

These standards apply to all areas of financial services, including financial planning, insurance, investing, estate planning, accounting, financial coaching, real estate, and mortgages.

 **To-do list:**

- List any changes in your life that require meeting with an advisor.
- Rate your happiness with your current advisory team.
- List any changes you need to make.
- _____
- _____

Positive Habit Maker							
Habit	S	M	T	W	T	F	S
Goals defined							
Educate yourself							
Think about how you think							
Relevancy to you							
Evaluate your options							
Assemble the pieces							
Detailed focus							
Yearly review							

THE BOTTOM LINE

Your advisor works for you, and if the relationship isn't working, then find an advisor who you are comfortable with and in whose services you are confident.

Review Your Support for the Next Generation

Sunday:	
Monday:	
Tuesday:	
Wednesday:	
Thursday:	
Friday:	
Saturday:	

The big picture: Follow a strategy that best meets your goals.
Why it matters: Providing financial support for your children, grandchildren, nieces, and nephews will help with the high costs of raising a child and getting an education.

What are your three big goals this week?

· Get Ready Goal: Review your support for the next generation.

· Goal 1: _____

· Goal 2: _____

Here's what works: Consider what strategy is right for you along with the amount of the gift. Parents will follow a different path than grandparents, aunts, and uncles. Here are three common methods:

· **Gifting:** You can give money directly to a minor, but a trust or a custodial account allows you to make gifts in the child's name, to be used for any expense for the benefit of the child. The custodial account should be established according to the Uniform Gift to Minors Act (UGMA) and the Uniform Transfer to Minors Act (UTMA).

· **College savings account:** College savings accounts are tax-advantaged plans designed to help parents finance higher education. There are two main types: 529 plans and education savings accounts (ESAs or Coverdell accounts). Both allow the account owner to set up investment accounts for a beneficiary while offering tax-deferred growth. All contributions must be in cash. There are differences in how they can be used, contribution limits, income restrictions, account continuation, passing of control from parent to child, ability to change beneficiary, and who is qualified to open them.

- **Direct payment of expenses:** You can pay directly for a child's education (e.g., a grandparent could pay for preschool).

Check-in: Enter general information in the table below about your current support for the next generation.

Strategy	Purpose	Recipient	Amount and frequency	Notes
Trust				
Custodial account				
Retirement assets				
529 college savings account				
Coverdell college savings account				
Direct payment of expenses				
Other				

To-do list:

- List any changes in your life, such as a new addition to the family.
- List any adjustments you want to make.
- List the advisors you will discuss this with.

- _____

- _____

Positive Habit Maker							
Habit	S	M	T	W	T	F	S
Goals defined							
Educate yourself							
Think about how you think							
Relevancy to you							
Evaluate your options							
Assemble the pieces							
Detailed focus							
Yearly review							

One more thing: Educate yourself on the tax and legal ramifications of each type of support.

THE BOTTOM LINE

There are many ways to provide financial support to the children in your life.

Quarter 1 Reflection

Sunday:

Monday:

Tuesday:

Wednesday:

Thursday:

Friday:

Saturday:

The big picture: Take a deep breath and think of all that you accomplished.

Why it matters: It's important to take time to reflect on positive progress and challenges overcome, and to celebrate your wins.

Check-in: Reflect on your progress with the Get Ready Habits.

- Habit 1: Goals defined
  - Were you able to meet your goals?
  - Were your goals realistic?
- Habit 2: Educate yourself
  - What were your biggest learnings?
  - Were you able to implement what you learned?
  - Did you check on the experience and bias from information sources?
- Habit 3: Think about how you think
  - Did you have a positive mindset?
  - Were you judgment-free with yourself?
- Habit 4: Relevancy to you
  - Did your decisions align with your values?
  - Were you able to customize products to fit your needs?
- Habit 5: Evaluate your options
  - Did you evaluate your options?
  - How did you do with monitoring expenses?
  - Did you look for hidden costs?
- Habit 6: Assemble the pieces
  - Do you understand how everything you reviewed over the last three months fits together?
  - Were you able to see what is missing?
  - Did you terminate any products or services that are no longer needed?

- Habit 7: Detailed focus
  - Did you take the time to review details?
  - Were you able to have balance?
  - Did you seek out a professional advisor when needed?

- Habit 8: Yearly review
  - Do you feel like you were able to keep things up to date recently?
  - Did you update products and services to reflect your life events?

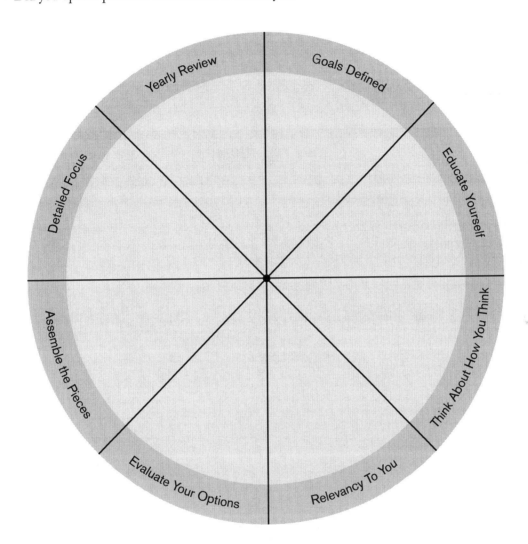

Here's what works: Continue to integrate the Get Ready Habits into your financial life. The Get Ready Habits empower you to take control of your financial life.

One more thing: Be gentle on yourself. If you didn't meet all of your goals, that's okay. It's all about the changes that you make going forward. Do the best that you can.

THE BOTTOM LINE

The Get Ready Habits empower you to take control of your financial life.

Monthly Reflection

What were your five biggest wins?

1.

2.

3.

4.

5.

ASK YOURSELF:

- How did the month go for you?
- What goals did you meet this month?
- What challenges did you overcome?
- How is your progress with the Get Ready Habits?
- How did you do with your habits?

- What were your biggest lessons learned?
- What were your insights this month?
- What tasks do you still need to work on?
- How will you improve next month?
- How will you celebrate your wins this month?

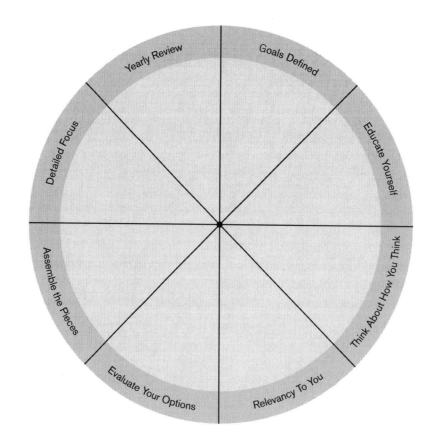

Expense Tracker			
Date	Payee	Category/Purpose	Amount

Cash Flow

MONTH 4

	Sunday	Monday	Tuesday	Wednesday	Thursday	Friday	Saturday
Week 14							
Week 15							
Week 16							
Week 17							

The big picture: Monitoring your cash flow allows you to see your income and expenses in one place.

Why it's important: Understanding your income and expenses will help you determine what changes may be needed.

Here's what works: This month we'll focus on these action items:

- Define your total income. Gather all of your income sources into one place.
- Review your expenses. Keeping an eye on your expenses will help you meet your goals.
- Create a cash flow statement. This helps you have all of your information in one place so you can make sure that you're not spending more than you make.
- Balance savings, expenses, and paying off debt. Review where your money goes.

ON THE CALENDAR

On the monthly calendar, write in the following items:

- The month and days
- Any fixed dates
- When you're expecting income
- Any bills due this month—mark the payment date seven days prior to the due date, along with the due date
- Life events
- Items from your to-do list

To-do list:

- Action steps to take this month
- Adjustments to make
- People to talk to
- Ways to make this month great
- Things you are looking forward to this month
- Distractions to avoid
- _____
- _____

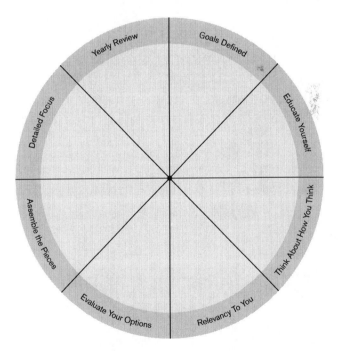

THE BOTTOM LINE

Understanding your cash flow will help you meet your goals.

Define Your Total Income

Sunday:
Monday:
Tuesday:
Wednesday:
Thursday:
Friday:
Saturday:

The big picture: Knowing your total income helps you with your overall planning.

Why it matters: Being able to live comfortably partially depends on how you manage your income. It helps you decide how much you can spend and how much you'll be able to save.

What are your three big goals this week?

· Get Ready Goal: Define your total income.

· Goal 1: _____

· Goal 2: _____

Here's what works: In the table below, calculate your total income, which includes wages, commissions, consulting fees, interest, dividends, capital gains, online sales, royalties, distributions, and more.

· Consider using gross income; your tax rate will vary from year to year, as well as by type of taxation (income tax, capital gains tax).

· Convert all of the income to annual; some of your income will come in different time increments (e.g., multiply your biweekly gross pay by 26 two-week periods in a year).

· You can use the detailed cash flow statement and budget in week 16 for a deeper dive.

One more thing: Consider how you can increase your income. In the weeks to come, we'll look at some ideas on how to do so.

Income source	Periodic amount	Periods in a year	Annual (calculate)	Notes (is this permanent, variable, and so on)
Example	$3,000	26	$78,000	Projected to be permanent
Primary occupation	$		$	
Other earned income	$		$	
Royalties	$		$	
Investment income	$		$	
Retirement income	$		$	
Rental income	$		$	
Other	$		$	
Total income	$		$	

- Research the average compensation for your position. Ask for a salary increase if you are underpaid. Know your value.
- Can you make more working somewhere else?

 **To-do list:**

- Add your total income to the year-end summary (see week 52).
- List any changes to your life that will impact your income.
- List any adjustments you can make, like asking for a salary increase.
- List anyone you will talk to about this.

- _____

- _____

Positive Habit Maker							
Habit	S	M	T	W	T	F	S
Goals defined							
Educate yourself							
Think about how you think							
Relevancy to you							
Evaluate your options							
Assemble the pieces							
Detailed focus							
Yearly review							

THE BOTTOM LINE

Knowing your total income is key to being in control of your financial life and helps you see the full picture.

Review Your Expenses

| Sunday: |
| Monday: |
| Tuesday: |
| Wednesday: |
| Thursday: |
| Friday: |
| Saturday: |

The big picture: A key to positive cash flow is to be mindful of expenses.

Why it matters: Monitoring your expenses will help you be a more informed consumer, reduce outlay, and get the most favorable pricing.

What are your three big goals this week?

· Get Ready Goal: Review your expenses.

· Goal 1: _____

· Goal 2: _____

Here's what works: Enter general totals for your current expenses in the table below.

· You can use the detailed cash flow statement and budget in week 16 for a deeper dive.

Name	Average monthly payment
Loans and debts	$
Utilities	$
Cable TV	$
Cell phone	$
Maintenance, cleaning, gardening	$
Childcare	$
Subscriptions and digital services	$
Taxes	$
Insurance premiums	$
Other	$
Total expenses	$

- Set up reminders for bills that you are expecting. Sometimes, bills get lost in the mail or lost in spam filters. If you create reminders, you'll not only know bills that are coming but also have an easier time of anticipating and preparing for that cost.
- Ask your service providers, such as cable and phone, for a better deal. Many will offer a better package or a lower rate when you tell them you are considering other options. Prices in these industries have a lot of flexibility, so it pays to shop around.
- Consider expenses you can eliminate. This includes terminating unnecessary subscriptions or memberships. Cutting a few subscriptions at $10 a month and a rarely used gym membership at $100 a month can quickly add up.

One more thing: One of the best ways to get a discount is to ask for it politely.

 To-do list:

- Add your total expenses to the year-end summary (see week 52).
- List any changes in your life that will impact your expenses.
- List any adjustments you will be making.
- List who you plan to talk to about this.
- _____
- _____

Positive Habit Maker							
Habit	S	M	T	W	T	F	S
Goals defined							
Educate yourself							
Think about how you think							
Relevancy to you							
Evaluate your options							
Assemble the pieces							
Detailed focus							
Yearly review							

THE BOTTOM LINE

Keeping an eye on your expenses will help you meet your goals.

Create a Cash Flow Statement

Sunday:	
Monday:	
Tuesday:	
Wednesday:	
Thursday:	
Friday:	
Saturday:	

The big picture: Know where your money is going.

Why it matters: Understanding your cash flow will help you see where your money is going. This information will guide you toward any changes that can be made.

What are your three big goals this week?

- Get Ready Goal: Create a cash flow statement.
- Goal 1: _____
- Goal 2: _____

Here's what works: Enter general totals in the table below. It's okay if you don't have all the information on your first go; you can make estimates and review.

- If you'd like to use a budget, enter your budgeted amounts and whether the category is over or under budget.
- You can use the detailed cash flow statement and budget below for a deeper dive.
- Review your cash flow (and budget) at least annually.
- If you have any significant changes to your income or your expenses, it's a good idea to update your cash flow statement.
- Be judgment-free on your cash flow. It's okay if you've made spending choices that need to be adjusted. What's important is what you do going forward. And, if you want to spend money on getting coffee out every day, that's okay, as long as you make other adjustments.

Category	Last year's total	This year's projected total	Budget	Over or under budget
Total income	$	$	$	$
Total expenses	$	$	$	$
Net cash flow (total income – total expenses)	$	$	$	$

One more thing: Budgets are a subject of much debate as to whether they are truly important to a sound financial plan. There are many websites and books that are dedicated strictly to budgeting, and budgeting is even part of most financial planning software. Ultimately, using (and sticking to) a budget is up to you. Whether or not you choose to use a budget, it's important to review your cash flow at least once a year.

To-do list:

· Add your net cash flow to the year-end summary (see week 52).
· List any changes in your life that may impact your cash flow, such as a job change.
· List any adjustments you will be making.
· List any advisors you will be talking to about this.

· _____

· _____

Positive Habit Maker							
Habit	S	M	T	W	T	F	S
Goals defined							
Educate yourself							
Think about how you think							
Relevancy to you							
Evaluate your options							
Assemble the pieces							
Detailed focus							
Yearly review							

THE BOTTOM LINE

Understanding your cash flow is an important aspect of organizing your financial life and meeting your goals.

Cash Flow Statement as of Date: _____

Income	Actual amount (annual)	Budgeted amount	Over or under amount
EARNED INCOME			
Cash compensation (primary job)	$	$	$
Second job (side job)	$	$	$
Online income/sales	$	$	$
Royalties (copyrights, trademarks, patents, other)	$	$	$
Other earned income	$	$	$
Subtotal: earned income	$	$	$
UNEARNED INCOME/INVESTMENT INCOME			
Checking, savings accounts	$	$	$
Stock dividends	$	$	$
Treasury securities	$	$	$
Bond(s) annual yield	$	$	$
Mutual fund dividends	$	$	$
Exchange-traded fund dividends	$	$	$
Royalties (copyrights, trademarks, patents, other)	$	$	$
Debt and obligations owed to you—interest	$	$	$
Other income	$	$	$
Reverse mortgage payout	$	$	$
Annuity distributions	$	$	$
Other unearned income	$	$	$
Subtotal: unearned income/investment income	$	$	$
RETIREMENT INCOME—THE INCOME YOU RECEIVE FROM YOUR RETIREMENT PLANS			
IRA	$	$	$
401(k), 403(b), and 457 plan(s)	$	$	$
Pension	$	$	$
Social Security	$	$	$
Other retirement income	$	$	$
Subtotal: retirement income	$	$	$
Total income	$	$	$

Expenses	Actual amount (annual)	Budgeted amount	Over or under amount
SAVINGS AND INVESTING			
Checking and savings account fees	$	$	$
Brokerage account fees	$	$	$
Investing fees	$	$	$
College savings account contributions	$	$	$
ABLE account contribution	$	$	$
Other savings and investing expenses	$	$	$
Flexible spending accounts	$	$	$
Subtotal: savings and investing	$	$	$
RETIREMENT SAVINGS—HOW MUCH IS SAVED UP IN A RETIREMENT ACCOUNT			
Individual retirement account (IRAs)	$	$	$
Self-employed and small business IRA(s)	$	$	$
401(k), 403(b), and 457 plan(s)	$	$	$
Other employer and group retirement plan(s)	$	$	$
Other retirement funding	$	$	$
Subtotal: retirement savings	$	$	$
LOANS AND DEBTS			
Loans	$	$	$
Car loan and lease payment(s)	$	$	$
Mortgage (primary residence) payment	$	$	$
Mortgage payment (HELOC and home equity)	$	$	$
Private mortgage insurance payment	$	$	$
Vacation home and time-share payment	$	$	$
Student loan payment(s)	$	$	$
Investment property payments	$	$	$
Business property loan payment(s) (commercial)	$	$	$
Personal debts and loan payment(s)	$	$	$
Credit card payment(s)	$	$	$
Debt consolidation loan payment(s)	$	$	$
Other loan payment(s)	$	$	$
Subtotal: loans and debts	$	$	$

continued...

Expenses	Actual amount (annual)	Budgeted amount	Over or under amount
UTILITY AND HOUSEHOLD EXPENSES			
Cable/satellite TV	$	$	$
Electric	$	$	$
Garbage	$	$	$
Gardener/landscaping	$	$	$
Gas	$	$	$
Heating oil/propane	$	$	$
Homeowners association	$	$	$
Home security (alarm company)	$	$	$
Housecleaning	$	$	$
HVAC	$	$	$
Internet access	$	$	$
Pest control	$	$	$
Phone (cellular)	$	$	$
Phone (landline)	$	$	$
Pool maintenance	$	$	$
Septic	$	$	$
Transit	$	$	$
Water/sewer	$	$	$
Other utility/household expenses	$	$	$
Subtotal: utility and household expenses	$	$	$
CARE AND SUPPORT—CHILDCARE, DAY CARE, TUITION, AND ADULT CARE			
Childcare	$	$	$
Day care	$	$	$
Tuition	$	$	$
Adult care	$	$	$
Other care and support expenses	$	$	$
Subtotal: care and support—childcare, day care, tuition, and adult care	$	$	$

Expenses	Actual amount (annual)	Budgeted amount	Over or under amount
SUBSCRIPTIONS AND DIGITAL SERVICES			
Newspapers (physical and digital)	$	$	$
Magazines and periodicals (physical and digital)	$	$	$
Cloud storage	$	$	$
General web services	$	$	$
Music streaming	$	$	$
Video streaming	$	$	$
Gaming	$	$	$
Food and delivery services	$	$	$
Software subscriptions	$	$	$
Membership sites	$	$	$
Other subscriptions and digital services	$	$	$
Subtotal: subscriptions and digital services	$	$	$
MEMBERSHIPS, SEASON TICKETS, CLUBS, AND ORGANIZATIONS			
Auto club (AAA)	$	$	$
Gym	$	$	$
Service club	$	$	$
Season tickets	$	$	$
Other	$	$	$
Subtotal: memberships, season tickets, clubs, and organizations	$	$	$
TAXES			
Income taxes (federal, state, local, Social Security)	$	$	$
Property taxes	$	$	$
Other taxes	$	$	$
Subtotal: taxes	$	$	$

continued...

Expenses	Actual amount (annual)	Budgeted amount	Over or under amount
INSURANCE			
Group insurance premiums	$	$	$
Auto insurance	$	$	$
Disability insurance	$	$	$
Health insurance	$	$	$
Health care costs	$	$	$
Homeowners/renters insurance	$	$	$
Life insurance	$	$	$
Long-term care insurance	$	$	$
Annuity premiums	$	$	$
Other insurance premiums	$	$	$
Subtotal: insurance	$	$	$
Total expenses	$	$	$

TOTAL CASH FLOW

(total net income – total expenses) $_____ – $_____ = $_____

Balance Savings, Expenses, and Debt Repayment

The big picture: It's important to balance paying off debt, paying your expenses, and saving for the future.

Why it matters: Knowing what debt to pay off, as well as meeting expenses, while also saving for the future is an important part of your planning. Finding balance will help you optimize your finances.

What are your three big goals this week?

- Get Ready Goal: Balance savings and paying off debt.
- Goal 1: _____
- Goal 2: _____

Here's what works: Create your budgeting ratio.

- Step 1: Net (after-tax) income divided by monthly essential expenses: _____ percent. Your essential expenses include housing costs, utilities, food, insurance, car payments, transportation, and other mandatory expenses.
- Step 2: Net income divided by monthly nonessential expenses: _____ percent. Nonessential expenses include dining out, shopping, entertainment, vacations, subscriptions, memberships, and anything else that is not essential.
- Step 3: Savings, investments, and debt: _____ percent. This is the net after tax income divided by savings, investments, and debt payoff.

What is it? Your budget ratio is step 1/step 2/step 3. Using a 50/30/20 budgeting ratio helps you allocate your monthly expenses among essential spending; nonessential spending; and savings, investing, and debt payoff.

Sunday:

Monday:

Tuesday:

Wednesday:

Thursday:

Friday:

Saturday:

Check-in: The 20 percent that's allocated to savings, investing, and debt payoff can be allocated as follows. This ratio is a benchmark, and you should adjust as needed to meet your goals.

- Focus on paying off high interest-rate debt.
- Contribute to a rainy day fund. In case of an unforeseen event, you may need immediate access to cash. Start with enough money to pay one month's rent.
- If your employer offers a 401(k) with a matching contribution, take advantage of the full match. This is a guaranteed return, whether your employer matches 50 percent or 100 percent of your contribution.

One more thing: Consider whether you can reasonably expect to invest your money with a higher return rate. For example, if you can reasonably expect a return of 6 percent on a mutual fund, you may not want to pay off a mortgage with a 3 percent interest rate. Keep in mind that this does not take into account tax issues such as whether your mutual funds will incur an income or capital gains tax and whether your mortgage interest is tax deductible. Also, mortgages are amortized, which means most of your payments go to interest and later payments to principal.

 To-do list:

- Add your budget ratio to the year-end summary (see week 52).
- List any changes in your life that may impact your balance. Examples include buying a house with a new mortgage or starting a job with a 401(k) employer match.
- List any adjustments you will make.
- List any advisors you need to discuss this with.

- _____

- _____

Positive Habit Maker							
Habit	S	M	T	W	T	F	S
Goals defined							
Educate yourself							
Think about how you think							
Relevancy to you							
Evaluate your options							
Assemble the pieces							
Detailed focus							
Yearly review							

THE BOTTOM LINE

Finding balance is key to ensuring that you can meet all of your goals and obligations.

Monthly Reflection

What were your five biggest wins?

1.

2.

3.

4.

5.

ASK YOURSELF:

- How did the month go for you?
- What goals did you meet this month?
- What challenges did you overcome?
- How is your progress with the Get Ready Habits?
- How did you do with your habits?

- What were your biggest lessons learned?
- What were your insights this month?
- What tasks do you still need to work on?
- How will you improve next month?
- How will you celebrate your wins this month?

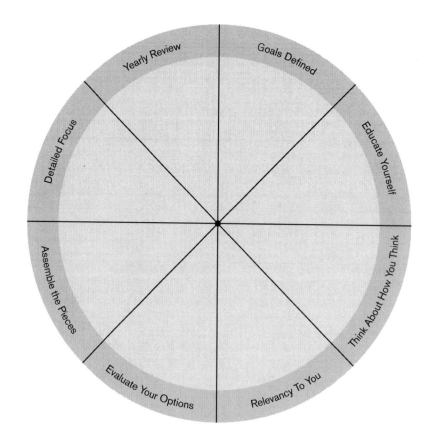

Expense Tracker

Date	Payee	Category/Purpose	Amount

Net Worth

MONTH 5

	Sunday	Monday	Tuesday	Wednesday	Thursday	Friday	Saturday
Week 18							
Week 19							
Week 20							
Week 21							

The big picture: Review your net worth so you have all of your assets and liabilities in one place.

Why it's important: Knowing your net worth helps you see if you are on track for a healthy financial life.

Here's what works: This month we'll focus on these action items:

- Review your checking and savings accounts. Your bank accounts are the foundation of your financial assets.
- Review your property and assets. Knowing the value of what you own will help you determine your net worth.
- Review your debts. This will help you minimize your payments and interest.
- Update your net worth statement. Your net worth statement is the total value of everything you own (your assets) less what you owe (your liabilities).

ON THE CALENDAR

On the monthly calendar, write in the following items:

- The month and days
- Any fixed dates
- When you're expecting income
- Any bills due this month—mark the payment date seven days prior to the due date, along with the due date
- Life events
- Items from your to-do list

 **To-do list:**

- Action steps to take this month
- Adjustments to make
- People to talk to
- Ways to make this month great
- Things you are looking forward to this month
- Distractions to avoid

- _____
- _____

Yearly Review

Goals Defined

Detailed Focus

Educate Yourself

Assemble the Pieces

Think About How You Think

Evaluate Your Options

Relevancy To You

THE BOTTOM LINE

Growing your net worth will allow you to meet your goals.

Review Your Checking and Savings Accounts

Sunday:

Monday:

Tuesday:

Wednesday:

Thursday:

Friday:

Saturday:

The big picture: Checking and savings accounts form the foundation of your financial life.

Why it matters: Checking and savings accounts provide a safe place to put your money and will help you start saving.

· Checking accounts allow you to make deposits, withdrawals, and transfers, as well as write checks. There are even some that pay interest. You will usually be provided with a debit or ATM card, along with a checkbook.

· Savings accounts are interest-earning deposit accounts and will usually pay a higher interest rate than a checking account.

What are your three big goals this week?

· Get Ready Goal: Review your checking and savings accounts.

· Goal 1: _____

· Goal 2: _____

Here's what works: Find the right checking and savings accounts to meet your goals and values.

· Institution type: You can choose between credit unions and a traditional bank. Credit unions require membership based on an association like an employer or a common group. Credit unions can be a good alternative to traditional banks.

· Branch location: If you will need to go to a physical location, make sure that there are branches near your home and work. Credit unions are often regional, which may be a factor if you travel a lot.

- Interest rates: Banks typically pay lower than the national average, while credit unions typically pay higher. Online banks also often pay a higher interest rate.
- Online and mobile banking: If you will be doing most of your banking online or with an app, check out what is offered. Smaller credit unions may not have great technology.
- Fees: Credit unions tend to have lower fees than banks.
- Loan interest rates: Credit unions tend to have lower interest rates than banks.
- Product offerings: Banks tend to offer more products.
- Customer service: Due to their size and commitment to investors, credit unions typically provide better service.
- High-yield savings accounts: These accounts can offer a substantially higher interest rate than traditional savings accounts. However, they may be harder to access.
- Deposit insurance: Verify that you have deposit insurance, which provides guarantees up to a specific amount, in the event your bank goes under. Banks should be members of the Federal Deposit Insurance Corporation (www.fdic.gov), and credit unions can participate in the National Credit Union Share Insurance Fund (www.ncua.gov/support-services/share-insurance-fund).

 To-do list:

- List any changes in your life that may impact your banking needs.
- List any adjustments you will be making.
- List who you will talk to about this.

- _____

- _____

Positive Habit Maker							
Habit	S	M	T	W	T	F	S
Goals defined							
Educate yourself							
Think about how you think							
Relevancy to you							
Evaluate your options							
Assemble the pieces							
Detailed focus							
Yearly review							

THE BOTTOM LINE

Monitor your checking and savings accounts to minimize your fees and maximize your interest rates.

Review Your Property and Assets

Sunday:
Monday:
Tuesday:
Wednesday:
Thursday:
Friday:
Saturday:

The big picture: Understanding what you own helps you see the big picture.

Why it matters: Everything we own has a specific value. Your property and assets help determine whether you are on track to meet your goals, including reaching financial independence (retirement).

What are your three big goals this week?

· Get Ready Goal: Review your property and assets.

· Goal 1: _____

· Goal 2: _____

Here's what works: Calculate the total value of everything that you own. This includes bank accounts, marketable securities and investments, retirement plans, residence, cars, real estate, jewelry, collectibles, and business interests.

· Estimate the fair-market value. It's okay to estimate as values are not constant; they are simply a snapshot in time. It's best to be conservative on the values.

· Include the total market value. Next week we'll review loans, so no need to include them here.

· To get an accurate value for your home, use something like www.zillow.com. To value your vehicles, use www.edmunds.com. Use conservative estimates on other items.

· Enter general information about your property and assets in the table below. You can use the detailed cash flow statement and budget in week 16 for a deeper dive.

	Estimated fair-market value	As of date	Notes
Bank accounts	$		
Liquid assets	$		
Investments	$		
Retirement plans	$		
Home	$		
Car	$		
Personal property	$		
Business interests	$		
Other	$		
Other	$		
Total	$		

To-do list:

- Add the total fair-market value of your property and assets to the year-end summary (see week 52).
- List any changes in your life that may impact your property and assets, such as a change in marital status or selling a business interest.
- List any adjustments you will be making.
- List who you are planning to discuss this with.

- _____

- _____

Positive Habit Maker							
Habit	S	M	T	W	T	F	S
Goals defined							
Educate yourself							
Think about how you think							
Relevancy to you							
Evaluate your options							
Assemble the pieces							
Detailed focus							
Yearly review							

THE BOTTOM LINE

Reviewing your property and assets helps you assemble your net worth statement.

Review Your Debts

Sunday:

Monday:

Tuesday:

Wednesday:

Thursday:

Friday:

Saturday:

The big picture: Reviewing your debts will help you minimize your payments and interest rates.

Why it matters: You may reduce your interest rates, extend guarantees, or pay off loans. Loan interest rates and terms can fluctuate with the market or your financial picture (credit score, income, etc.).

What are your three big goals this week?

· Get Ready Goal: Review your debts.

· Goal 1: _____

· Goal 2: _____

Here's what works: Inventory your debts using the table below.

· You can use the detailed net worth statement in week 21 for a deeper dive.

Next, calculate your debt-to-income ratio (DTI):

· Step 1: Total monthly debt payments:
  $_____

· Step 2: Total monthly gross income:
  $_____

· Step 3: Debt-to-income ratio (step 1/step 2): ____ percent

What is it? The debt-to-income ratio measures the percentage of your household income spent on paying off debt. Lenders use this metric to determine your ability to repay loans.

Lenders prefer the debt-to-income ratio to be 36 percent or less. If you live in an area where homes are very expensive, your DTI may be significantly higher. Keep your DTI as low as possible; this will help you get lower rates and avoid being seen as a borrowing risk.

Debt type	Lender	Loan balance	Interest rate	Monthly payments
Mortgage		$		$
Auto loan		$		$
Student loan		$		$
Credit card 1		$		$
Credit card 2		$		$
Credit card 3		$		$
Other		$		$
Other		$		$
Total		$		$

- Make all loan payments in full when they are due to avoid late payment charges and negative impact on your credit history and credit score.
- Because credit cards have high interest rates, pay your balances in full and do not carry any balance.
- Always pay more than the minimum balance due on a credit card or similar debt. If you pay only the minimum balance due, it will take you many years to pay off that loan.
- Check whether any loans changed interest rate or other terms.
- Pay off your highest-interest-rate debt as quickly as possible and then work your way to paying off your lowest-interest-rate debt.
- Check with your lender and other lenders to see if you're eligible for a lower interest rate or better guarantees.
- If you're offered a reduced monthly payment, make sure that it's due to a lower interest rate rather than the payment period being extended.
- If you're restructuring any of your loans, be sure to consider any refinancing charges.

To-do list:

- Add your debt-to-income ratio to the year-end summary (see week 52).
- List any changes in your life that will impact your debts.
- List any adjustments you will be making.
- List who you plan to talk to about this.

- _____

- _____

Positive Habit Maker							
Habit	S	M	T	W	T	F	S
Goals defined							
Educate yourself							
Think about how you think							
Relevancy to you							
Evaluate your options							
Assemble the pieces							
Detailed focus							
Yearly review							

THE BOTTOM LINE

Take control of your debt portfolio so you can minimize your loan expenses.

Update Your Net Worth Statement

The big picture: Creating a net worth statement brings all of your information together.

Why it matters: Knowing your net worth will help you determine whether you are financially solvent and on track for a healthy financial life and retirement.

What is it? Your net worth is the total value of everything that you own (assets) less what you owe (liabilities).

What are your three big goals this week?

- Get Ready Goal: Create your net worth statement.

- Goal 1: _____

- Goal 2: _____

Here's what works: Take the total value of your assets that you calculated in week 19 and subtract the total value of your debts and liabilities from week 20. This is your net worth. See the Net Worth Statement below for an in-depth review, but here's the basic formula:

- Week 19 (assets) total: $_____ – Week 20 (liabilities) total: $_____ = Net worth: $_____

Check-in: Create your net worth ratio.

- Step 1: Annual gross income (from all sources): $_____

- Step 2: Age: _____

- Step 3: Multiply your annual gross income by your age: $_____

- Step 4: Net worth ratio (step 3/step 1): _____

The sum (step 4) should equal your net worth. Your earning power will be impacted by the choices you make; for example, if you went for an advanced educational degree, you

Sunday:	
Monday:	
Tuesday:	
Wednesday:	
Thursday:	
Friday:	
Saturday:	

will be starting work later but will expect to have higher future earnings. This ratio is from the book *The Millionaire Next Door*.[1]

Consider what change you can make to increase your net worth. This can either be increasing income or decreasing debt.

 **To-do list:**

· Add your net worth and net worth ratio to the year-end summary (see week 52).
· List any changes in your life that will impact your net worth, such as a new mortgage.
· List any adjustments you can make.
· List who you will talk to about this.

· _____

· _____

Positive Habit Maker							
Habit	S	M	T	W	T	F	S
Goals defined							
Educate yourself							
Think about how you think							
Relevancy to you							
Evaluate your options							
Assemble the pieces							
Detailed focus							
Yearly review							

THE BOTTOM LINE

Your mission is to have more assets than liabilities and to grow your net worth.

---

1 Thomas J. Stanley and William D. Danko, *The Millionaire Next Door: The Surprising Secrets of America's Wealthy* (Lanham: Taylor Trade Publishing, 1996).

Net Worth Statement

Assets (what you own)	Fair-market value (estimated)
CASH AND LIQUID ASSETS	
Cash (at home—safe, wallet, etc.)	$
Checking account(s)	$
Savings account(s)	$
Certificate of deposit (CDs)	$
Money market account(s)	$
Annuity (surrender value)	$
Life insurance (surrender value)	$
Other liquid assets	$
Subtotal: cash and liquid assets	$
INVESTED ASSETS	
Brokerage accounts	$
Stock	$
Treasury securities	$
Bonds	$
Mutual funds	$
Exchange-traded funds (ETFs)	$
Collectibles	$
Stock options	$
Business interests/ownerships	$
Royalties value (copyrights, trademarks, patents, other)	$
Debt and obligations owed to you	$
College savings accounts	$
ABLE accounts	$
Other assets	$
Subtotal: invested assets	$

continued...

Assets (what you own)	Fair-market value (estimated)
RETIREMENT ASSETS	
Individual retirement accounts (IRA & Roth IRA)	$
Self-employed and small business plans (Keogh, SEP-IRA, SARSEP IRA, SIMPLE IRA, "solo" 401(k), and a defined-benefit plan)	$
401(k), 403(b), and 457 plan(s)	$
Pension lump sum benefit (vested amount)	$
Other employer and group retirement plan(s)	$
Other retirement accounts	$
Subtotal: retirement assets	$
PROPERTY	
Home (primary residence)	$
Vacation home (secondary residence)	$
Investment property	$
Farmland	$
Undeveloped land	$
Commercial property	$
Car(s)	$
Planes, boats, and recreational vehicles	$
Computers	$
Entertainment (TVs and stereos)	$
Appliances	$
Other	$
Subtotal: property	$
Total assets	$

Liabilities	Fair-market value (estimated)
CURRENT LIABILITIES	
Auto loan(s)	$
Credit card(s)	$
Life insurance policy loan	$
Student loan	$
Other short-term loan	$
Subtotal: current liabilities	$
LONG-TERM LIABILITIES	
Mortgage (primary residence)	$
Second mortgage	$
Home equity loan (HELOC)	$
Vacation home and time-share loan balance(s)	$
Reverse mortgage balance	$
Investment property loan balance(s)	$
Business property loan balance(s) (commercial)	$
Personal debts and loan balance(s)	$
Debt consolidation loan balance(s)	$
Other loan balance(s)	$
Subtotal: long-term liabilities	$
Total liabilities	$
Net worth (total assets minus total liabilities)	$

Monthly Reflection

What were your five biggest wins?

1.

2.

3.

4.

5.

ASK YOURSELF:

- How did the month go for you?
- What goals did you meet this month?
- What challenges did you overcome?
- How is your progress with the Get Ready Habits?
- How did you do with your habits?

- What were your biggest lessons learned?
- What were your insights this month?
- What tasks do you still need to work on?
- How will you improve next month?
- How will you celebrate your wins this month?

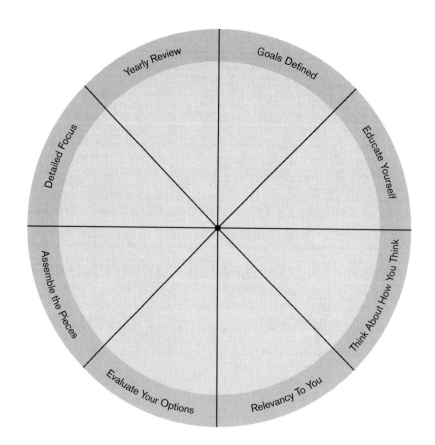

Expense Tracker

Date	Payee	Category/Purpose	Amount

Strategy Review

MONTH 6

	Sunday	Monday	Tuesday	Wednesday	Thursday	Friday	Saturday
Week 22							
Week 23							
Week 24							
Week 25							
Week 26							

The big picture: Review your money strategies.

Why it's important: Having strategies in place will help you meet your goals. This includes savings, investment, and tax planning.

Here's what works: This month we'll focus on these action items:

- Review your savings strategy. Have a plan to make sure that you're saving money.
- Check your rainy day fund. Make sure that you have sufficient money put aside for unforeseen events, whether it's a car repair or an emergency.
- Review your Investment Policy Statement. Review your roadmap for how you will invest your money. Stick to your plan.
- Prepare for income taxes. Make sure that you have all of the tax documents that you need. And be sure to consider how you can legally minimize your taxes.

 **ON THE CALENDAR**

On the monthly calendar, write in the following items:

- The month and days
- Any fixed dates
- When you're expecting income
- Any bills due this month—mark the payment date seven days prior to the due date, along with the due date
- Life events
- Items from your to-do list

To-do list:

- Action steps to take this month
- Adjustments to make
- People to talk to
- Ways to make this month great
- Things you are looking forward to this month
- Distractions to avoid
- _____
- _____

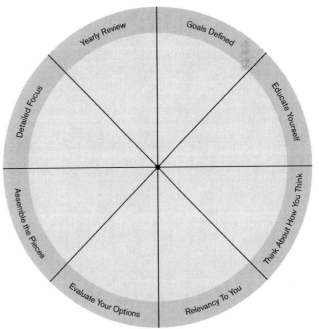

THE BOTTOM LINE

Having a strategy for your money will help you get to your goals.

Review Your Savings Strategy

Sunday:	
Monday:	
Tuesday:	
Wednesday:	
Thursday:	
Friday:	
Saturday:	

The big picture: Have a plan for saving money.

Why it matters: Saving money for the future is how you will meet your goals such as creating a safety net fund, buying a home, and achieving financial independence.

What are your three big goals this week?

· Get Ready Goal: Review your savings strategy.

· Goal 1: _____

· Goal 2: _____

Here's what works: In the table below, enter in how much you're saving for your goals. It's okay to estimate.

	Amount per year	Notes
Liquidity fund	$	
Short-term goals	$	
Medium-term goals	$	
Long-term goals	$	
Other goals	$	
Total for all goals	$	

Check-in: Create your savings ratio. It is an easy way to see how much of your income you are saving.

· Step 1: Gross annual income: $_____ (from week 14)

· Step 2: Total annual savings: $_____

· Step 3: Divide annual savings by annual income (step 2/step 1): _____

Your savings ratio should be between 12 percent and 20 percent. This ratio has a wide range; it depends on your current age, your desired age for financial independence (retirement), and how much you've already saved.

- Set your savings goals with timelines and priority.
- Determine what percentage of income or flat amount will go to your savings goals.
- Put your money into savings after you've paid your necessary expenses.
- Your savings should be allocated into accounts that match your goals (e.g., if your goal is for a safety net fund, put the money into a liquid account, where you can immediately access the money).
- Set up an automatic transfer of a flat amount to a savings or investment account for each pay statement.
- Monitor your savings rate to determine whether you need to save more.

To-do list:

- Add your savings ratio to the year-end summary (see week 52).
- Are there any changes in your life that may impact your savings strategy?
- Will you be making any adjustments to your savings strategy?
- Who will you be discussing this with?

- _____

- _____

Positive Habit Maker							
Habit	S	M	T	W	T	F	S
Goals defined							
Educate yourself							
Think about how you think							
Relevancy to you							
Evaluate your options							
Assemble the pieces							
Detailed focus							
Yearly review							

THE BOTTOM LINE

Pay yourself first by having a plan for how much of your earnings will go to savings.

Check Your Rainy Day Fund

Sunday:

Monday:

Tuesday:

Wednesday:

Thursday:

Friday:

Saturday:

The big picture: A rainy day fund helps protect you against an unexpected event.

Why it matters: Having cash reserves provides liquidity for financial challenges such as a loss of income, unforeseen medical expense, or vital car repair.

What are your three big goals this week?

· Get Ready Goal: Check your rainy day fund.

· Goal 1: _____

· Goal 2: _____

Here's what works: Calculate your liquidity ratio so you can see if you are on track with your rainy day fund. The liquidity ratio is how many months of cash you have available in the event of a rainy day event.

· Step 1: Add up your fixed monthly expenses (housing, insurance, utilities, car payments, food, etc.):
$_____.

· Step 2: Add up your liquid cash (this is money that is immediately available such as from your checking account and savings account): $_____.

· Step 3: Divide available liquid cash by fixed monthly expenses (step 2/step 1): $_____.

A good benchmark is to save enough to cover three to six months of essential expenses. Your rainy day fund should remain liquid and should not be invested. When you need it, you'll want to make sure that you won't have any surrender charges or other barriers to accessing your money.

- Consider opening a separate high-yield savings account (with an FDIC-insured bank or credit union) if you feel like you might be tempted to use the money in a current bank account.
- To reach a desired threshold (three to six months of expenses), start by adding a little to your emergency account each month.
- Set up an automatic transfer from your main bank account to your rainy day fund.

 To-do list:

- Add your liquidity ratio to the year-end summary (see week 52).
- Make any adjustments to meet your rainy day goal.
- List any changes in your life that may impact your rainy day fund.
- Talk to your financial planner or financial coach; they can help you set up and adjust your rainy day fund.

Positive Habit Maker							
Habit	S	M	T	W	T	F	S
Goals defined							
Educate yourself							
Think about how you think							
Relevancy to you							
Evaluate your options							
Assemble the pieces							
Detailed focus							
Yearly review							

THE BOTTOM LINE

There is no magic number. Just put aside what you feel will protect you if you were to lose your income for an extended period, usually three to six months of expenses.

Review Your Investment Policy Statement

Sunday:

Monday:

Tuesday:

Wednesday:

Thursday:

Friday:

Saturday:

The big picture: An Investment Policy Statement is your roadmap to managing your investment portfolio.

Why it matters: Your Investment Policy Statement can help you transition from being an investment collector to an organized investor. Being organized will keep you focused on the big picture.

What are your three big goals this week?

· Get Ready Goal: Review your Investment Policy Statement.

· Goal 1: _____

· Goal 2: _____

Here's what works: Review your Investment Policy Statement on the following pages. Here's what to consider in each area during your future annual reviews.

· **Goals:** Have there been any changes?

· **Investment strategy:** Recommended to not change unless there is a good reason. Don't chase "hot" sectors.

· **Risk tolerance:** As you get older, this will change, and it's usually recommended that you take on less risk as you get older, especially when approaching retirement or in retirement. When you're younger, you can wait out market volatility; however, fluctuations in riskier investments will have a greater impact on your overall portfolio at a later stage.

· **Asset allocation:** This is how your investments are divided up. And this should be adjusted if your risk tolerance level has changed.

- **Investment criteria:** Is there a new type of investment that makes sense for your portfolio? This would not be a risky new investment like cryptocurrency; rather, it might be a new type of index investing. For example, when exchange traded funds (ETFs) were introduced, they became a good alternative to mutual funds. Your criteria should be in line with your investment strategy.
- **Investment balances:** Gathering your current information allows you to view your current asset totals and their percentages of your portfolio. It also allows you to include new investments and remove old ones.
- **Rebalancing guideline:** Rebalance when the allocations are outside your target allocation range.
- **Review:** Adjust your investments as necessary.

One more thing: When you get investment advice or tips, keep in mind whether the source is qualified and whether they are biased.

 To-do list:

- List any changes in your life that will impact your Investment Policy Statement.
- List any adjustments you need to make.
- List the advisors you will discuss this with.

- _____

- _____

Positive Habit Maker							
Habit	S	M	T	W	T	F	S
Goals defined							
Educate yourself							
Think about how you think							
Relevancy to you							
Evaluate your options							
Assemble the pieces							
Detailed focus							
Yearly review							

THE BOTTOM LINE

Reviewing your Investment Policy Statement will keep you focused on the big picture, so you can easily see how everything is working and if adjustments are needed.

Investment Policy Statement

An Investment Policy Statement will help you transition from being an investment collector to becoming an organized investor. Being organized will keep you focused on the big picture rather than being concerned about short-term market changes.

STEP 1: DEFINE YOUR OBJECTIVES

The Investment Policy Statement is a roadmap to managing your investment portfolio. You'll assemble an overview of your goals, objectives, asset allocation, risk tolerance, and investment philosophy.

The following seven steps will guide you through creating your Investment Policy Statement (on the last page).

Note: Please be advised that I am not an investment advisor, and this is not investment advice. Please consult a qualified investment advisor when applicable.

Identify your short-term and long-term financial goals, such as paying off debt, saving for college, starting a business, saving for retirement, retirement income distribution, and leaving an inheritance. Your goals should be realistic, specific, and important to you. They may also offset each other, so you may need to prioritize your goals.

Reaching your goals will depend on a number of factors:

- Your time horizon for funding your goals
- The length of time that you will be withdrawing funds (e.g., 30 years for retirement, four years for college)
- The amount of money that you will need

STEP 2: OUTLINE YOUR INVESTMENT STRATEGY

This is the foundation for your Investment Policy Statement. Set clear principles for the statement. This helps keep you on course with your personal investment philosophy. Here are some questions to consider:

- Do you plan to be an active investor or passive investor (high maintenance vs. low maintenance)?
- Are low-cost investments important to you? For example, do you want to use low-expense index funds?
- Do you want actively managed funds or passively managed funds?
- Are dividends a goal? And if yes, will you reinvest them?
- Will you be keeping a long-term strategy rather than a short-term strategy? Avoid timing the market.

Example

Here's my Investment Policy Statement strategy:

- I maintain a diversified, low-maintenance, low-expense investment portfolio.
- I maintain my investments in both bull and bear markets and I will not try to time the market.

Manage your fees and expenses. This is one of the best things you can do for your investment portfolio. If you can save 1 percent on your annual fees and expenses, that is an additional 1 percent gain for your portfolio. This is often easier said than done, as many fees and expenses are not clearly disclosed or easy to understand. If you can't understand something, you shouldn't buy it.

STEP 3: IDENTIFY YOUR RISK TOLERANCE

Investing involves a relationship between risk and reward. All types of investments include some level of risk. The theory is that your potential for a greater investment return increases as you take on more risk. It's important that you understand that you could lose some or all of the money you invest and that you may not always get a higher return with a higher level of risk.

High vs. low risk

- If you have a higher risk tolerance level, you may be able to handle a higher level of risk in your portfolio. This can include a higher percentage of stocks and riskier asset classes such as commodities or currencies.
- If you have a lower risk tolerance level, your investment portfolio would consist of a higher level of bonds and cash with a lower level of stocks.

Impact of your time horizon

You may also have different levels of risk tolerance for specific goals and time horizons. For example, your level of risk tolerance will decrease as you approach retirement or if you have a short-term goal.

Discover your risk tolerance level

A risk tolerance questionnaire will help you gauge your risk tolerance level. There are many risk tolerance questionnaires available on the web that may provide you with a suggested asset allocation based on your responses to different scenarios. The companies that provide the questionnaires may have a bias toward their own products and services. Here are two risk tolerance questionnaires:

- Investor Profile Questionnaire (Schwab: www.schwab.com/resource/investment-questionnaire)
- Investment Risk Tolerance Quiz (Rutgers: www.njaes.rutgers.edu/money/assessment-tools/investment-risk-tolerance-quiz.pdf)

STEP 4: SET YOUR ASSET ALLOCATION LIMITS

Asset allocation is about how much of your money is invested in a specific category of investment (stocks, bonds, cash, and other asset classes). Asset classes move differently under different market conditions.

Diversifying your assets will lower the volatility of your investment portfolio.

Asset allocation targets and rebalancing ranges

- Stocks, bonds, cash, and other broad asset target allocations
- Large-cap, small-cap, international, and other detailed asset target allocations
- Timing for altering these allocations
- Minimum and maximum range that would lead to portfolio rebalancing

Here are two asset allocation calculators that can help you:

- Investment Allocation Calculator (Calcxml: www.calcxml.com/do/inv01)
- Funds Investment Questionnaire (Vanguard: https://investor.vanguard.com/tools-calculators/investor-questionnaire#modal-start-quiz)

STEP 5: INVESTMENT SELECTION CRITERIA

Determine criteria and apply them to each investment. Carefully consider investments that don't pass your criteria test. This will help you to stay focused on your longer-term strategy. Investment selection criteria could include the following:

- Low-cost (expense ratio) mutual funds and ETFs.
- Actively managed funds will have higher turnover and distributions than passive management funds (e.g., index funds).
- How risky is the investment? Minimize the market risk.
- Shelter tax-inefficient funds in tax-advantaged accounts.
- Avoid actively managed funds, commodities, and cryptocurrencies.
- Use a ratings system, such as Morningstar or Standard and Poor's Ratings. Personally, I use Schwab's rating system and only buy securities with an A or B rating. Many investment firms have their own proprietary ratings system.

STEP 6: DOCUMENT YOUR CURRENT INVESTMENTS

It's important to have all of your investment information in one place. You can quickly review them and make adjustments to fit your Investment Policy Statement. Be sure to contact an investment advisor if you are uncertain about the impact of selling (taxes, penalties, other restrictions).

Having all of your documents organized will help you prepare tax returns, apply for a loan, be prepared for an emergency, and make sure that your spouse and children have access to all your investments if you are unable to handle your affairs.

Your inventory should include the account name, account number, investment name, current value, cost basis, number of shares (amount), and access information (website and log-in credentials).

STEP 7: REVIEW AND REBALANCE

It's important to set a schedule to review your investments. Review them at least yearly. Major life changes should include a quick review of your investments. Those events include birth, death, marriage, divorce, occupation change, and graduation.

During your review process, assess whether your investments meet your Investment Policy Statement criteria. Adjust your investments as necessary. Here's what to consider:

- Have there been any changes to your objectives?
- Do not change your investment strategy unless there is a good reason. Avoid chasing "hot" sectors.
- As you get older, your risk tolerance level will change, and it's usually recommended that you take on less risk as you get older, especially when approaching retirement or in retirement, when fluctuations in riskier investments will have a greater impact on your overall portfolio.
- If your risk tolerance level has changed, then you should adjust your asset allocation.
- Is there a new type of investment that makes sense for your portfolio? This would not be a risky new investment like cryptocurrency; rather, it might be a new type of index investing. For example, when ETFs were introduced, they became a good alternative to mutual funds. Your criteria should be in line with your investment strategy.
- Gathering your current information allows you to view current asset totals and percentages of your portfolio. It also allows you to include new investments and remove old investments.
- Rebalance when your allocations are outside your target allocation range.

Over time, your investments will no longer be in line with your allocations. This is natural because some investments will gain in value while others decrease in value. Rebalancing ensures that your portfolio is in line with your Investment Policy Statement.

Rebalancing may create taxable events and incur transaction fees, so be sure to review investments within each asset allocation category. Rebalancing may involve selling off investments from an overweighted investment category and purchasing investments in an underweighted category. Your financial advisor can help you minimize these costs. You may also have access to automated portfolio rebalancing through your investment firm.

Investment Policy Statement

Goals and objectives for your investment programs **Example goal: Financial independence** • Timeline: Retire at age 65 • Amount needed: $1 million • For how long: 30 years	**Goal 1:** • Timeline: • Amount needed: • For how long: **Goal 2:** • Timeline: • Amount needed: • For how long: **Goal 3:** • Timeline: • Amount needed: • For how long:
Investment strategy	Example: buy and hold lowest cost investments
Risk questionnaire used: Outcome:	
Asset allocation targets	Stocks: _____% to _____% US large-cap: _____% to _____% US mid-cap: _____% to _____% US small-cap: _____% to _____% Foreign equities: _____% to _____% Bonds: _____% to _____% Short-term: _____% to _____% Intermediate-term: _____% to _____% Long-term: _____% to _____% Real estate: _____% to _____% Cash: _____% to _____% Other: _____: _____% to _____%
Investment selection criteria	
Investment summary	Taxable accounts: $_____ Qualified (retirement accounts): $_____ Other: _____: $_____
Review and rebalance	Frequency: _____ Rebalance when allocations to asset classes are _____ % points from targets
Notes:	

Prepare for Income Taxes

The big picture: Tax preparedness is for everyone, not just the wealthy.

Why it matters: You can minimize your taxes by preparing for income taxes.

What are your three big goals this week?

- Get Ready Goal: Prepare for income taxes.
- Goal 1: _____
- Goal 2: _____

Here's what works: Check to see that you receive all your necessary tax documents on time.

- Always save your tax documents and receipts, including charitable donations, so you can take all available deductions.
- Review all tax forms. If they are inaccurate or anything is missing, contact the issuer immediately for a correction.
- Review your tax returns carefully to ensure you are maximizing all of your deductions. This includes using tax-advantaged retirement accounts and college savings accounts.
- File your taxes on time. See the Fixed Dates chapter.
- Request an extension if necessary. States follow different rules, so check with the tax authority in your state to avoid fines and penalties for missing deadlines. Keep in mind that an extension to file is not an extension to pay taxes. If you owe taxes, you should pay them before the due date to avoid potential penalties and interest on the amount owed.

Sunday:

Monday:

Tuesday:

Wednesday:

Thursday:

Friday:

Saturday:

- Determine whether you may need to pay estimated taxes as a result of under-withholding or being self-employed. See the Fixed Dates chapter for their deadlines.

One more thing: If you receive a paycheck, it's a good idea to use the IRS Withholding Calculator to perform a quick paycheck checkup. The calculator helps you make sure you have the right amount of tax withheld from your paycheck.

- Checking your withholding can help protect against having too little tax withheld and facing an unexpected tax bill or penalty at tax time next year.

To-do list:

- List any changes in your life that will impact your taxes, such as a change in marital status or new kid.
- List any adjustments you need to make.
- List who you will be discussing this with.

- _____

- _____

Positive Habit Maker							
Habit	S	M	T	W	T	F	S
Goals defined							
Educate yourself							
Think about how you think							
Relevancy to you							
Evaluate your options							
Assemble the pieces							
Detailed focus							
Yearly review							

THE BOTTOM LINE

Being prepared for taxes will help you make sure that you are paying the right amount.

Quarter 2 Reflection

The big picture: Take a deep breath and think of all that you accomplished.

Why it matters: It's important to take time to reflect on positive progress and challenges overcome, and to celebrate your wins.

Check-in: Reflect on your progress with the Get Ready Habits.

- Habit 1: Goals defined
  - Were you able to meet your goals?
  - Were your goals realistic?

- Habit 2: Educate yourself
  - What were your biggest learnings?
  - Were you able to implement what you learned?
  - Did you check on the experience and bias from information sources?

- Habit 3: Think about how you think
  - Did you have a positive mindset?
  - Were you judgment-free with yourself?

- Habit 4: Relevancy to you
  - Did your decisions align with your values?
  - Were you able to customize products to fit your needs?

- Habit 5: Evaluate your options
  - Did you evaluate your options?
  - How did you do with monitoring expenses?
  - Did you look for hidden costs?

- Habit 6: Assemble the pieces
  - Do you understand how everything you reviewed over the last three months fits together?
  - Were you able to see what is missing?
  - Did you terminate any products or services that are no longer needed?

Sunday:

Monday:

Tuesday:

Wednesday:

Thursday:

Friday:

Saturday:

- Habit 7: Detailed focus
  - Did you take the time to review details?
  - Were you able to have balance?
  - Did you seek out a professional advisor when needed?
- Habit 8: Yearly review
  - Do you feel like you were able to keep things up to date recently?
  - Did you update products and services to reflect your life events?

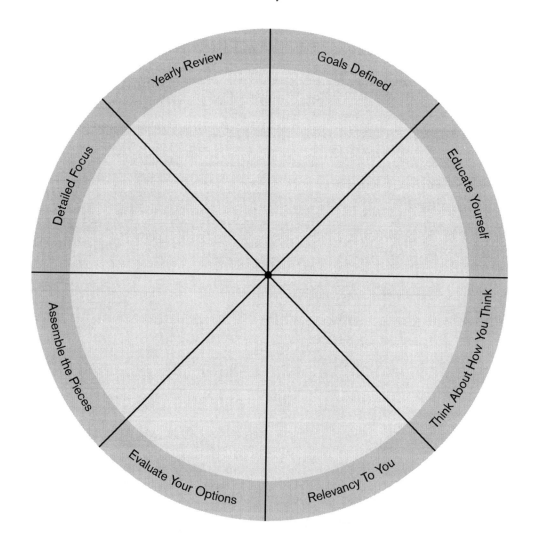

Here's what works: Continue to integrate the Get Ready Habits into your financial life. The Get Ready Habits empower you to take control of your financial life.

One more thing: Be gentle on yourself. If you didn't meet all of your goals, that's okay. It's all about the changes that you make going forward. Do the best that you can.

THE BOTTOM LINE

The Get Ready Habits empower you to take control of your financial life.

Monthly Reflection

What were your five biggest wins?

1.

2.

3.

4.

5.

ASK YOURSELF:

- How did the month go for you?
- What goals did you meet this month?
- What challenges did you overcome?
- How is your progress with the Get Ready Habits?
- How did you do with your habits?

- What were your biggest lessons learned?
- What were your insights this month?
- What tasks do you still need to work on?
- How will you improve next month?
- How will you celebrate your wins this month?

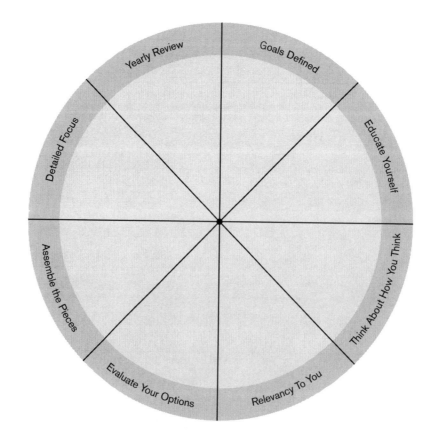

Expense Tracker

Date	Payee	Category/Purpose	Amount

Are You Protected?

MONTH 7						
Sunday	Monday	Tuesday	Wednesday	Thursday	Friday	Saturday
Week 27						
Week 28						
Week 29						
Week 30						

The big picture: Make sure that you are protecting your potential risks.

Why it's important: Insurance is the base of a sound financial plan. If you are faced with a loss, insurance will provide coverage rather than you having an out-of-pocket loss.

Here's what works: This month we'll focus on these action items:

- Review your auto insurance. Make sure that you have the right coverage and are taking advantage of discounts.
- Review your homeowners and renters insurance. Make sure that coverage is up to date and that you are taking advantage of discounts.
- Review your health and Medicare insurance. Check to see if your providers and medications are covered, as well as whether you can make changes to your plan to lower your premium.
- Review your disability insurance. If you are dependent on your income, make sure that you have the right amount of disability insurance.

ON THE CALENDAR

On the monthly calendar, write in the following items:

- The month and days
- Any fixed dates
- When you're expecting income
- Any bills due this month—mark the payment date seven days prior to the due date, along with the due date
- Life events
- Items from your to-do list

To-do list:

- Action steps to take this month
- Adjustments to make
- People to talk to
- Ways to make this month great
- Things you are looking forward to this month
- Distractions to avoid

- _____

- _____

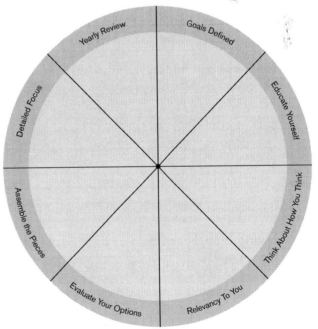

THE BOTTOM LINE

Be protected by having the appropriate types and amounts of insurance.

Review Your Auto Insurance

Sunday:	
Monday:	
Tuesday:	
Wednesday:	
Thursday:	
Friday:	
Saturday:	

The big picture: Review your auto insurance to make sure you have the right coverage and eligible discounts.

Why it matters: If you purchased the minimum coverage required by law or chose the policy without guidance, you may not have all of the coverage you need.

- Insurance companies offer a range of discounts if you meet requirements. Make sure that you're getting all of the discounts that you're eligible for.

What are your three big goals this week?

- Get Ready Goal: Review your auto insurance.
- Goal 1: _____
- Goal 2: _____

Here's what works: Reevaluate your needs and then compare to your coverages, including the deductibles, exclusions, and coverage limits. If you're driving fewer miles, you might be eligible for a lower rate (usually less than 7,500 miles per year).

- Make sure your information is accurate and up to date. Your car insurance company will determine your rates based on factors including your age, location, and annual mileage.
- Compare the policy renewal with your existing policy to catch any changes in coverage or price. If there are changes, call your insurer to find out why.
- Are there any changes on your policy renewal?
- Raise the deductible on collision and comprehensive coverages. If you have an old car with a low cash value, you might want to drop these coverages altogether. Will you be raising the deductible? If so, add this to your to-do list.

- Report your safety devices, which can result in discounts up to 25 percent.
- Pay premiums annually. Insurance companies have "convenience" fees for nonannual premium payments. You can save up to 10 percent by paying annually. If you plan to change your payment frequency, add this to your to-do list.
- You may receive a discount for bundling multiple policies from one company (from 5 percent to 20 percent). Will you be looking into bundling your policies? If so, add this to your to-do list.

One more thing: A good time to check out other options is about 90 days before your policy renewal. Choose the policy that offers the best value. Do not focus on price alone but on the amount of coverage offered for that price. Compare items such as deductibles, exclusions, and coverage limits.

- Each insurance company uses its own method to calculate your premium. Premiums depend on several key factors, including driving record, age, gender, marital status, type of vehicle, where you live, vehicle annual use, and previous claims.

To-do list:

- List any changes in your life that may impact your auto insurance, such as a new driver.
- List any changes you plan to make.
- List who you will be discussing this with.

- _____

- _____

Positive Habit Maker							
Habit	S	M	T	W	T	F	S
Goals defined							
Educate yourself							
Think about how you think							
Relevancy to you							
Evaluate your options							
Assemble the pieces							
Detailed focus							
Yearly review							

THE BOTTOM LINE

Reviewing your auto insurance helps you have the right coverage at the lowest premium.

Review Your Homeowners and Renters Insurance

Sunday:

Monday:

Tuesday:

Wednesday:

Thursday:

Friday:

Saturday:

The big picture: The key for homeowners and renters insurance is to know exactly what is covered.

Why it matters: Having the right coverage will make sure that you are fully protected in the event of a claim. Homeowners and renters insurance policies may not cover everything that you expect them to and will differ in how coverages may be defined.

What are your three big goals this week?

· Get Ready Goal: Review your homeowners and renters insurance.

· Goal 1: _____

· Goal 2: _____

Here's what works: Calculate the replacement cost of your home:

· Step 1: Square footage of your home: _____

· Step 2: Average cost per square foot to rebuild: $_____

· Step 3: Multiply the square footage of your home by the average cost per square foot to rebuild (step 1 × step 2): $_____

The costs to rebuild vary significantly across the country, so consider contacting an appraiser or contractor. Your insurance agent or insurance company can also provide an estimate using a replacement cost calculator.

· Usually, the property and its contents are covered for the named perils. If you have an all-risk policy, every event is covered except for listed exclusions.

· Increasing your deductible will lower your premium.

- You may be able to get a lower premium if your home has safety features like dead-bolt locks, smoke detectors, an alarm system, storm shutters, or fire-retardant roofing material; if you are 55 years of age or older; or if you are a long-term customer.
- After a disaster, the land under your house is still there. If you do not subtract the value of the land when deciding how much homeowners insurance to buy, you will pay more than you should.
- Get replacement coverage, not an "actual cash value" policy. Purchase enough coverage to replace what is insured so you will have enough money to rebuild your home and replace its contents. An "actual cash value" policy is cheaper but pays only what your property is worth at the time of loss—your cost minus depreciation for age and wear.
- Ask about any special coverage you might need, such as for special property like computers, cameras, jewelry, art, antiques, musical instruments, and stamp collections. Home contents are usually reimbursed only up to 50 percent of the home's insured value, unless listed separately.

One more thing: Earthquake and floods are not typically covered under homeowners and renters insurance policies. Coverage may be obtained by adding an endorsement or purchasing a standalone policy. Visit www.riskfactor.com to check out your risk from flooding, wildfire, and heat from climate change.

 To-do list:

- List any changes in your life that might impact your homeowners insurance, such as a renovation or addition.
- List your insurance agent's contact information if you will talk to them about this.

- _____

- _____

Positive Habit Maker							
Habit	S	M	T	W	T	F	S
Goals defined							
Educate yourself							
Think about how you think							
Relevancy to you							
Evaluate your options							
Assemble the pieces							
Detailed focus							
Yearly review							

THE BOTTOM LINE

Reviewing your homeowners and renters insurance makes sure that you have the coverage you need.

Review Your Health and Medicare Insurance

Sunday:

Monday:

Tuesday:

Wednesday:

Thursday:

Friday:

Saturday:

The big picture: Review your options so you have the optimal coverage at the lowest cost.

Why it matters: There are a variety of options for health insurance, including Medicare, that you should review to make sure that you have the coverage you need with the optimal deductible.

What are your three big goals this week?

· Get Ready Goal: Review your health and Medicare insurance.

· Goal 1: _____

· Goal 2: _____

Check-in: Calculate your total true health care cost.

· Step 1: Annual premium: $_____

· Step 2: Annual co-pays and coinsurance: $_____

· Step 3: Deductible: $_____

· Step 4: Out-of-pocket health care expenses: $_____

· Step 5: Add up steps 1–4: $_____ (total health care cost)

What is this? This is how much your total annual health care bill is. At open enrollment, you can try out different premium and deductible options to see if you can reduce your total health care cost.

Here's what works: Be prepared for open enrollment since it's generally the only time of year where you can make changes to your Medicare plans. There are special enrollment periods if you have a qualifying life event. Here's what to consider at open enrollment:

- Review your plan for changes to provider networks. Have there been any changes to your provider's network?
- Decide whether you need to change your deductible and co-pays. There is no set-in-stone formula for calculating your deductible; sometimes insurance companies will price in an "incentive" for a certain deductible, so determining your break-even point is always a good idea. Ask yourself whether the money you save in insurance premiums justifies taking on a higher risk, along with a higher deductible (and with health insurance, higher co-pays and coinsurance).

One more thing: Check your open enrollment date and add it to your calendar.

To-do list:

- List any changes in your life that will impact your health care costs.
- List any adjustments you need to make to your health or Medicare insurance at open enrollment or in a special enrollment period.
- List who you will be talking to about this.
- _____
- _____

Positive Habit Maker							
Habit	S	M	T	W	T	F	S
Goals defined							
Educate yourself							
Think about how you think							
Relevancy to you							
Evaluate your options							
Assemble the pieces							
Detailed focus							
Yearly review							

THE BOTTOM LINE

Health insurance plans including Medicare have a wide variety of options, so be sure you have the right coverage.

Review Your Disability Insurance

Sunday:

Monday:

Tuesday:

Wednesday:

Thursday:

Friday:

Saturday:

The big picture: Is your income protected in the event of a short-term or long-term disability?

Why it matters: Your chances of becoming disabled for more than 90 days before the age of 65 are quite high, ranging from close to 50 percent at age 30, to 40 percent at age 45.

- The average length of disability ranges from 78 months (ages 30–34) to 86 months (ages 45–49).
- The probability of disability lasting five years or more is 35 percent (ages 30–34) to 43 percent (ages 45–49).

What are your three big goals this week?

- Get Ready Goal: Review your disability insurance.
- Goal 1: _____
- Goal 2: _____

Check-in: Determine your current income protection from disability insurance (individual disability insurance and group long-term disability insurance) in the table below.

Here's what works: Purchase individual disability income insurance, if needed. Disability policies may be issued with an exclusion for a certain illness or injury, which can be removed after a certain period. For example, if you have knee surgery, the insurance company may exclude any disabilities related to the knee for a certain period of time. You will need to file a request to have this exclusion removed; the insurance company will not usually remove it automatically.

- Know the terms of any future-purchase or future-increase options and be sure to take advantage if you are eligible. Your insurance company may or may not notify you.

	Notes	Example numbers	Your numbers
Monthly income needed if disabled	Expenses and investment funding for financial independence, college, etc.	$7,000	$
Income that would continue if disabled	Passive income, etc.	$500	$
Disability insurance needed	Income needed minus income that would continue	$6,500	$
Current individual disability insurance	Total monthly benefit	$1,000	$
Group LTD current coverage	Monthly gross income (usually base salary) multiplied by the percentage of income covered (usually 50%–60%)	$8,000 monthly salary at 50% coverage = $4,000	$
Group LTD monthly benefit	Apply any maximum benefit cap (typical on group LTD policies)	Cap: $5,000 – benefit under cap	$
Group LTD net after tax benefit	If pretax benefit, your gross income tax rate—typically 35%–40%	$4,000 pretax benefit – 35% tax rate = $2,600	$
Group LTD needed	Disability insurance need – (LTD net after tax benefit + current individual disability insurance benefit)	$6,500 (needed) – ($1,000 individual + $2,600 group) = $2,900 needed	$
Disability insurance ratio	Coverage held / coverage needed	$3,600 current / $6,500 needed = 55%	$

To-do list:

- Add your disability insurance ratio to the year-end summary (see week 52).
- List any changes in your life that may impact your disability insurance needs such as a new job or launching a business.
- List any adjustments you need to make to your disability insurance.
- List who you will be discussing this with. Consider talking to a disability insurance specialist.
- _____
- _____

Positive Habit Maker							
Habit	S	M	T	W	T	F	S
Goals defined							
Educate yourself							
Think about how you think							
Relevancy to you							
Evaluate your options							
Assemble the pieces							
Detailed focus							
Yearly review							

THE BOTTOM LINE

If you are dependent upon your income, you need to protect it.

Monthly Reflection

What were your five biggest wins?

1.

2.

3.

4.

5.

ASK YOURSELF:

- How did the month go for you?
- What goals did you meet this month?
- What challenges did you overcome?
- How is your progress with the Get Ready Habits?
- How did you do with your habits?

- What were your biggest lessons learned?
- What were your insights this month?
- What tasks do you still need to work on?
- How will you improve next month?
- How will you celebrate your wins this month?

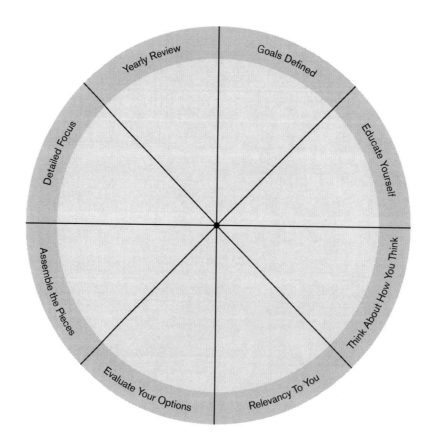

Expense Tracker

Date	Payee	Category/Purpose	Amount

Your Legacy

MONTH 8

	Sunday	Monday	Tuesday	Wednesday	Thursday	Friday	Saturday
Week 31							
Week 32							
Week 33							
Week 34							

The big picture: Making a plan will protect your legacy.

Why it's important: Have a plan in place to make sure that your money and assets go where you want them to go, as well as to make sure that your wishes are known in the case of a major health event.

Here's what works: This month we'll focus on these action items:

- Review beneficiaries. It's important to keep beneficiaries updated to ensure that your assets go where you want them to go.
- Review your wills and trusts. Wills and trusts allow you to choose who receives your assets when you pass away.
- Review your powers of attorney and directives. Make sure that these are in place and you've discussed this with your agents.
- Review your life insurance. Determine whether you have the right amount and type of life insurance.

📅 ON THE CALENDAR

On the monthly calendar, write in the following items:

- The month and days
- Any fixed dates
- When you're expecting income
- Any bills due this month—mark the payment date seven days prior to the due date, along with the due date
- Life events
- Items from your to-do list

📋 To-do list:

- Action steps to take this month
- Adjustments to make
- People to talk to
- Ways to make this month great
- Things you are looking forward to this month
- Distractions to avoid

- _____
- _____

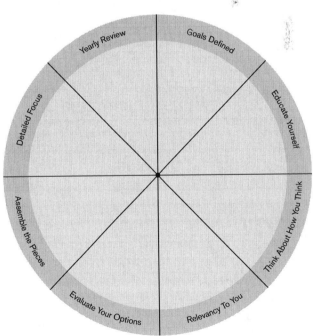

THE BOTTOM LINE

Protect your legacy by following a plan.

Review Beneficiaries

Sunday:
Monday:
Tuesday:
Wednesday:
Thursday:
Friday:
Saturday:

The big picture: By reviewing and designating beneficiaries, you can ensure that when the time comes your assets will go exactly where you specify.

Why it matters: Beneficiary designations take priority over wills and trusts, so if, for example, an ex-spouse is still your named beneficiary, they will receive the proceeds.

· You can designate beneficiaries on investment accounts, retirement plans, bank accounts, life insurance policies, wills, trusts, and more.

What are your three big goals this week?

· Get Ready Goal: Review your beneficiary designations.

· Goal 1: _____

· Goal 2: _____

Check-in: Add in current beneficiary designations in the table.

Here's what works: By reviewing and designating beneficiaries annually or when you have a major life event, you can ensure that, when the time comes, your assets will go exactly where you specify. If you don't name a beneficiary, your assets may be distributed through the terms of your will, pass through probate, and be distributed based on intestacy law.

· Name a contingent beneficiary in the event that your primary beneficiary predeceases you. Consider naming a nonprofit organization if you would prefer that they receive the money.

One more thing: If needed, consult with a qualified tax advisor or attorney. There are tax consequences that go with naming a trust as the beneficiary for your retirement plan and annuities.

Type	Name of plan	Primary beneficiary	Contingent beneficiary	Note
Will				
Trust				
Checking account				
Savings account				
Life insurance (individual)				
Life insurance (group–employer)				
IRA				
401(k) or 403(b)				
Other				
Other				

To-do list:

- List any life events that impact your beneficiary status, such as a change in marital status or the birth of a child.
- List any changes you will be making.
- List who you plan to discuss this with.
- _____
- _____

Positive Habit Maker							
Habit	S	M	T	W	T	F	S
Goals defined							
Educate yourself							
Think about how you think							
Relevancy to you							
Evaluate your options							
Assemble the pieces							
Detailed focus							
Yearly review							

THE BOTTOM LINE

Your beneficiary designations and not your will dictate what will happen to your life insurance, retirement plans, and other assets that have beneficiary designations.

Review Your Wills and Trusts

Sunday:
Monday:
Tuesday:
Wednesday:
Thursday:
Friday:
Saturday:

The big picture: Wills and trusts allow you to choose who receives your assets when you pass away.

Why it matters: If you die without a will, your property will be distributed under the intestacy laws of the state where you reside.

What are your three big goals this week?

· Get Ready Goal: Review your wills and trusts.

· Goal 1: _____

· Goal 2: _____

Check-in: Enter information in the following table about your will and trusts, including location.

Here's what works: Keep your will and trusts up to date to ensure that your assets are distributed according to your current wishes.

· Be sure to share the location of the documents with your executor. If no one knows the documents exist, they may not be acted on.

· Work with a qualified estate planning attorney to ensure that your plan is done properly.

One more thing: Your estate plan cannot be changed after you die, so be sure to review on a regular basis.

To-do list:

· Add the location of your estate planning documents to the year-end summary (see week 52).

Estate planning document	Full title	Date of document	Location of document	Executor or trustee	Notes
Will					
Living trust					
Other					
Other					

- List any changes in your life that may impact your estate planning, such as a change in marital status or new dependent.
- If you had a child turn 18, you should update your estate planning documents to reflect that they are now an adult.
- List any changes you will be making.
- List who you plan to talk to about this, such as an attorney.

- _____

- _____

Positive Habit Maker							
Habit	S	M	T	W	T	F	S
Goals defined							
Educate yourself							
Think about how you think							
Relevancy to you							
Evaluate your options							
Assemble the pieces							
Detailed focus							
Yearly review							

THE BOTTOM LINE

Reviewing your will and trusts will make sure that everything is up to date and in accordance with your wishes.

Review Your Powers of Attorney and Directives

Sunday:

Monday:

Tuesday:

Wednesday:

Thursday:

Friday:

Saturday:

The big picture: Powers of attorney and directives allow you to appoint someone to make legal, financial, and health care decisions in case you are not able to do so, even if it's for a limited period.

Why it matters: When there is no power of attorney or advanced care directive in place, your wishes may not be followed.

What are your three big goals this week?

· Get Ready Goal: Review your powers of attorney and directives.
· Goal 1: _____
· Goal 2: _____

Check-in: In the table below, enter information about your powers of attorney and directives.

Here's what works: Create a financial power of attorney and an advanced health care directive.

· Be sure to discuss your powers of attorney and directives with your agents. If they don't know the documents exist or what your wishes are, they will not be able to meet your goals.

 **To-do list:**

· Add the location of your powers of attorney and directives to the year-end summary (see week 52).
· List any changes in your life that may require you to update your powers of attorney and directives, such as a change in marital status.

Document type	Full title	Document date	Location of document	Agent	Notes
Power of attorney (durable)					
Power of attorney (nondurable)					
Health care or advanced care directive					
Other					
Other					

- List any adjustments you need to make.
- List who you will talk to about this.

- _____

- _____

Positive Habit Maker							
Habit	S	M	T	W	T	F	S
Goals defined							
Educate yourself							
Think about how you think							
Relevancy to you							
Evaluate your options							
Assemble the pieces							
Detailed focus							
Yearly review							

THE BOTTOM LINE

Make sure that you have powers of attorney and directives in place to guarantee that your wishes are followed.

Review Your Life Insurance

Sunday:	
Monday:	
Tuesday:	
Wednesday:	
Thursday:	
Friday:	
Saturday:	

The big picture: Make sure you have just the right amount and type of life insurance.

Why it matters: If someone is financially dependent on you, then you need life insurance. If no one is dependent on you, you have no need for life insurance.

What are your three big goals this week?

· Get Ready Goal: Review life insurance.

· Goal 1: _____

· Goal 2: _____

Check-in: Create your life insurance ratio.

· Step 1: How much annual income would need to be replaced, if you were to pass away? $_____

· Step 2: What do you feel is a conservative rate of return that the death benefit be invested at? _____ (4–5 percent is reasonable)

· Step 3: Total coverage needed: divide annual income needed by the rate of return (step 1/step 2): $_____

· Step 4: Total current life insurance: $_____

· Step 5: Life insurance needed (total coverage needed – current total coverage): $_____

· Step 6: Life insurance coverage ratio (step 5/step 4): _____

What is this? Your life insurance ratio will help you determine whether your coverage matches your need. If your ratio is below 1, consider getting more life insurance. If your ratio is over 1, consider terminating some coverage.

Here's what works: Determine your need for life insurance.

- Consider how long you will need life insurance and purchase a policy for that time period. For example, if your spouse is dependent on your income until you reach financial independence (retirement), purchase a policy for that length of time. A smart strategy is to purchase different length policies for different needs.
- If your need for life insurance is for a specific period of time, then consider a term-life policy.
- If you have a permanent need for life insurance, consider a permanent-life policy, such as whole-life insurance or guaranteed universal life insurance. While there are other types of permanent life such as variable life and indexed universal life insurance, they are more complex.
- If you have a permanent life insurance policy, you should order an in-force illustration every two to three years. Permanent life insurance policies are made up of various components that impact policy performance, including earnings (interest rates, dividends, and so on), mortality costs, cost of insurance charges, and expense charges. An in-force illustration projects future performance of a life insurance policy using current values rather than the projections at the time of the policy issue. In-force illustrations are the only way to find out whether your life insurance policy is performing as expected.

 To-do list:

- Add your life insurance ratio to the year-end summary (see week 52).
- List any changes in your life that may impact your life insurance needs, such as a change in marital status or a new child.
- List any changes you will be making.
- List who you plan to talk to about this.

- _____

- _____

Positive Habit Maker							
Habit	S	M	T	W	T	F	S
Goals defined							
Educate yourself							
Think about how you think							
Relevancy to you							
Evaluate your options							
Assemble the pieces							
Detailed focus							
Yearly review							

THE BOTTOM LINE

Having the right amount and type of life insurance will ensure that those who depend on your income will be taken care of—no more and no less.

Monthly Reflection

What were your five biggest wins?

1.

2.

3.

4.

5.

ASK YOURSELF:

- How did the month go for you?
- What goals did you meet this month?
- What challenges did you overcome?
- How is your progress with the Get Ready Habits?
- How did you do with your habits?

- What were your biggest lessons learned?
- What were your insights this month?
- What tasks do you still need to work on?
- How will you improve next month?
- How will you celebrate your wins this month?

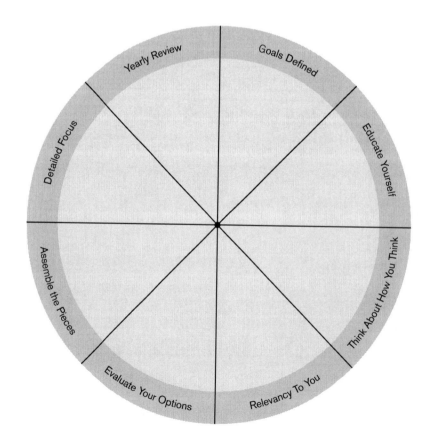

Expense Tracker

Date	Payee	Category/Purpose	Amount

Financial Independence

MONTH 9

	Sunday	Monday	Tuesday	Wednesday	Thursday	Friday	Saturday
Week 35							
Week 36							
Week 37							
Week 38							
Week 39							

The big picture: Consider what financial independence looks like to you.

Why it's important: We each have our own definition of financial independence. Reaching financial independence requires following a plan.

Here's what works: This month we'll focus on these action items:

- Review your Social Security statement. Social Security can be the foundation in our later years.
- Check your retirement plans. These plans are a great way to save money for financial independence.
- Maximize your passive income. You'll need a sufficient passive income stream if you plan to retire before you're eligible for money from retirements and Social Security.
- Check that you're on track for financial independence. Monitor your progress so you can make adjustments, if any need to be made.

ON THE CALENDAR

On the monthly calendar, write in the following items:

- The month and days
- Any fixed dates
- When you're expecting income
- Any bills due this month—mark the payment date seven days prior to the due date, along with the due date
- Life events
- Items from your to-do list

To-do list:

- Action steps to take this month
- Adjustments to make
- People to talk to
- Ways to make this month great
- Things you are looking forward to this month
- Distractions to avoid

- _____
- _____

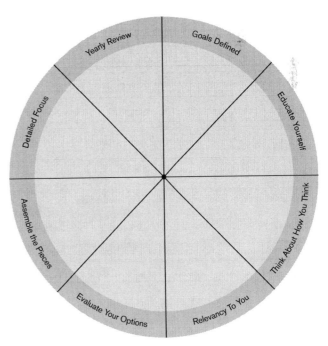

THE BOTTOM LINE

We can all reach financial independence if we have a plan that we follow.

Review Your Social Security Statement

Sunday:	
Monday:	
Tuesday:	
Wednesday:	
Thursday:	
Friday:	
Saturday:	

The big picture: Social Security provides income after a certain age.

Why it matters: Social Security is a federal government program that provides a source of income for you or your legal dependents (spouse, children, or parents) if you qualify for benefits.

- While you work, you pay Social Security taxes. This tax money goes into a trust fund that pays benefits to those who are currently retired, to people with disabilities, and to the surviving spouses and children of workers who have died.

- Each year you work, you'll get credits to help you become eligible for benefits when it's time for you to retire. You'll need 40 credits to be eligible for benefits on your individual work history.

- Your Social Security benefit statement indicates how much you or your family would receive in disability, survivor, or retirement benefits. It also includes a record of your lifetime earnings.

What are your three big goals this week?

- Get Ready Goal: Review your Social Security statement.
- Goal 1: _____
- Goal 2: _____

Check-in: Order your Social Security statement through the Social Security website: www.ssa.gov.

Here's what works: Review this statement for accuracy as your benefits are based on the record of lifetime earnings.

- If anything is inaccurate on your statement, contact Social Security to rectify. Any error could impact your Social Security benefit.

One more thing: Choosing when to take Social Security payments is an important decision, with numerous pros and cons. You can elect to take Social Security before your full "official" retirement age; however, you will receive a lower monthly benefit. The longer you wait to take Social Security, the higher the monthly benefit will be.

- Social Security is designed to be actuarially neutral, which means you are supposed to get about the same total amount of money no matter what age you file (i.e., you're paid less over a longer period if you file early).
- Your official retirement age depends on the year you were born. It appears on your Social Security statement, or you can use a Social Security calculator (www.consumerfinance.gov/retirement/before-you-claim) to determine the optimal age to file for Social Security.

 To-do list:

- List any changes in your life that may impact your plans.
- List any adjustments you want to make.
- List who you will talk to about this.

- _____

- _____

Positive Habit Maker							
Habit	S	M	T	W	T	F	S
Goals defined							
Educate yourself							
Think about how you think							
Relevancy to you							
Evaluate your options							
Assemble the pieces							
Detailed focus							
Yearly review							

THE BOTTOM LINE

Social Security benefits are not intended to be your only source of income when you retire. On average, Social Security will replace about 40 percent of your annual preretirement earnings. You will need other savings, investments, pensions, or retirement accounts to make sure you have enough money to live comfortably when you retire.

Check Your Retirement Plans

| Sunday: |
| Monday: |
| Tuesday: |
| Wednesday: |
| Thursday: |
| Friday: |
| Saturday: |

The big picture: Retirement plans are a key component in your journey to financial independence.

Why it matters: Retirement plans are used to plan for traditional retirement.

- Retirement accounts, with the exception of Roth IRAs, allow you to make contributions on a tax-free basis up to a certain amount.
- Retirement account values grow on a tax-deferred basis. In other words, you don't pay taxes until you take money out of a retirement account.

What are your three big goals this week?

- Get Ready Goal: Check your retirement plans.
- Goal 1: _____
- Goal 2: _____

Check-in: Enter the current balance and contribution information for your retirement plans in the table below.

Plan type	Balance	Annual contribution	Notes
Traditional IRAs	$	$	
Roth IRAs	$	$	
401(k), 403(b), 457	$	$	
Pension plan (lump sum balance)	$	$	
Other	$	$	
Other	$	$	
Total retirement plans balance	$	$	

Here's what works: Participate in employer-sponsored programs such as 401(k)s and 403(b)s.

- Don't miss out on your employer's match to your 401(k) or 403(b). This is essentially free money, which many people fail to collect. This matching contribution can be a set dollar amount or a percentage of your contribution.
- If you don't have access to an employer-sponsored program, you can contribute to an IRA or a Roth IRA.
- If you are self-employed or have a small business, you can set up a wide variety of retirement plans, including a Keogh, SEP-IRA, SARSEP IRA, SIMPLE IRA, "solo" 401(k), and defined benefit plan.

To-do list:

- Add your retirement plans balance to the year-end summary (see week 52).
- List any changes in your life that may impact your retirement planning such as a change in your work life.
- List any adjustments you need to make to your contributions.
- _____
- _____

Positive Habit Maker							
Habit	S	M	T	W	T	F	S
Goals defined							
Educate yourself							
Think about how you think							
Relevancy to you							
Evaluate your options							
Assemble the pieces							
Detailed focus							
Yearly review							

THE BOTTOM LINE

Taking full advantage of your retirement plans options are a great way to accumulate money on a tax-advantaged basis.

Maximize Your Passive Income

Sunday:
Monday:
Tuesday:
Wednesday:
Thursday:
Friday:
Saturday:

The big picture: Passive income is a great way to supplement and diversify your income.

Why it matters: Passive income is income that is generated in the future, from either limited activity or past activity. Basically, it's income where you are not actively performing tasks.

- The IRS defines passive income as "any rental activity or any business in which the taxpayer does not materially participate."
- Side hustles can generate passive income.

What are your three big goals this week?

- Get Ready Goal: Maximize your passive income.
- Goal 1: _____
- Goal 2: _____

Check-in: Calculate your total passive income and your passive income ratio.

- Total royalties (copyrights, trademarks, patents, and other property that can be licensed): $_____.
- Total rental income: $_____. This may not be completely passive if you are spending time managing and maintaining the property.
- Total investment income (capital gains, dividends, etc.): $_____.
- Total limited partnership income (including passive business interests): $_____.
- Total side hustle income: $_____.
- Total passive income: $_____ (add up from above).
- Total income: $_____ (from week 14).
- Passive income ratio (passive income/total income): _____.

What is it? The passive income ratio reflects how much of your income comes from passive income streams. The higher the ratio, the less dependent you are on your earned income. If the ratio is higher than 1, you are earning more from your passive income than your earned income.

To-do list:

- Add your passive income ratio to the year-end summary (see week 52).
- List any changes in your life that may impact your passive income.
- List any adjustments you will be making.
- List who you will discuss this with.

- _____

- _____

Positive Habit Maker							
Habit	S	M	T	W	T	F	S
Goals defined							
Educate yourself							
Think about how you think							
Relevancy to you							
Evaluate your options							
Assemble the pieces							
Detailed focus							
Yearly review							

THE BOTTOM LINE

Creating a passive income stream can provide a steady income stream that supplements your earned income stream.

Check that You're on Track for Financial Independence

Sunday:

Monday:

Tuesday:

Wednesday:

Thursday:

Friday:

Saturday:

The big picture: We need to reframe our thinking around the word *retirement*, because what we're really talking about is when we will be financially independent.

Why it matters: We each have our own definition of when we will "retire" from the workforce. Most people do not fully retire exactly when they reach age 65. There is no standard definition for what retirement really is.

What are your three big goals this week?

· Get Ready Goal: See if you are on track for financial independence.

· Goal 1: _____

· Goal 2: _____

Check-in: Estimate the amount of money you'll need in retirement below.

The 4 percent withdrawal rule is based on William Bengen's study "Determining Withdrawal Rates Using Historical Data." This number has been revised both up and down, so keep in mind that this is an estimate.

What is it? The financial independence ratio helps you determine whether you are financially independent. If your ratio is below 1, decide what changes you'll need to make. If your ratio is over 1, congratulations; you are most likely on track to be financially independent.

Here's what works: Consider what financial independence looks like to you.

· Determine how much income you'll need to support whatever path you follow.

Document type	Example	Amounts	Notes
Retirement plan balance	$500,000	$	
Estimated annual income from retirement plans (balance above × 4%)	$20,000 ($50,000 × .04)	$	
Social Security estimated income	$18,000 ($1,500 monthly benefit)	$	
Pension plan estimated income	$12,000 ($1,000 a month)	$	
Other retirement plan income	$6,000 ($500 a month from IRA)	$	
Other income from investments	$6,000 ($500 a month)	$	
Passive income	$0	$	
Other income	$0	$	
Total income	$70,000	$	
Income needed in retirement	$96,000 ($8,000 a month)	$	
Financial independence ratio (income needed in retirement / total income)	72% ($70,000 / $96,000)	___%	

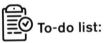 **To-do list:**

- Add your financial independence ratio to the year-end summary (see week 52).
- List any changes in your life that may impact your journey to financial independence.
- List any adjustments you need to make.
- List who you will discuss this with.

- _____

- _____

Positive Habit Maker							
Habit	S	M	T	W	T	F	S
Goals defined							
Educate yourself							
Think about how you think							
Relevancy to you							
Evaluate your options							
Assemble the pieces							
Detailed focus							
Yearly review							

THE BOTTOM LINE

Determine whether you are on track for what you define as financial independence.

Quarter 3 Reflection

The big picture: Take a deep breath and think of all that you accomplished.

Why it matters: It's important to take time to reflect on positive progress and challenges overcome, and to celebrate your wins.

Check-in: Reflect on your progress with the Get Ready Habits.

- Habit 1: Goals defined
  - Were you able to meet your goals?
  - Were your goals realistic?
- Habit 2: Educate yourself
  - What were your biggest learnings?
  - Were you able to implement what you learned?
  - Did you check on the experience and bias from information sources?
- Habit 3: Think about how you think
  - Did you have a positive mindset?
  - Were you judgment-free with yourself?
- Habit 4: Relevancy to you
  - Did your decisions align with your values?
  - Were you able to customize products to fit your needs?
- Habit 5: Evaluate your options
  - Did you evaluate your options?
  - How did you do with monitoring expenses?
  - Did you look for hidden costs?
- Habit 6: Assemble the pieces
  - Do you understand how everything you reviewed over the last three months fits together?
  - Were you able to see what is missing?
  - Did you terminate any products or services that are no longer needed?

Sunday:

Monday:

Tuesday:

Wednesday:

Thursday:

Friday:

Saturday:

- Habit 7: Detailed focus
  - Did you take the time to review details?
  - Were you able to have balance?
  - Did you seek out a professional advisor when needed?
- Habit 8: Yearly review
  - Do you feel like you were able to keep things up to date recently?
  - Did you update products and services to reflect your life events?

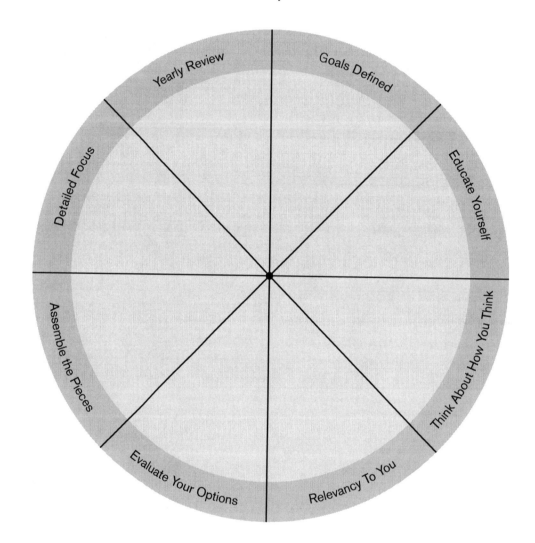

Here's what works: Continue to integrate the Get Ready Habits into your financial life. The Get Ready Habits empower you to take control of your financial life.

One more thing: Be gentle on yourself. If you didn't meet all of your goals, that's okay. It's all about the changes that you make going forward. Do the best that you can.

THE BOTTOM LINE

The Get Ready Habits empower you to take control of your financial life.

Monthly Reflection

What were your five biggest wins?

1.

2.

3.

4.

5.

ASK YOURSELF:

- How did the month go for you?
- What goals did you meet this month?
- What challenges did you overcome?
- How is your progress with the Get Ready Habits?
- How did you do with your habits?

- What were your biggest lessons learned?
- What were your insights this month?
- What tasks do you still need to work on?
- How will you improve next month?
- How will you celebrate your wins this month?

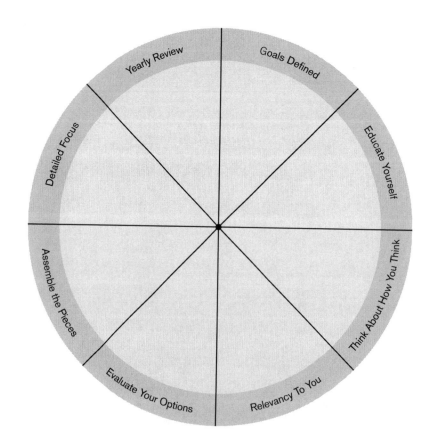

Expense Tracker

Date	Payee	Category/Purpose	Amount

Find Value

MONTH 10

	Sunday	Monday	Tuesday	Wednesday	Thursday	Friday	Saturday
Week 40							
Week 41							
Week 42							
Week 43							

The big picture: Make your money go further by getting the best value.

Why it's important: When you save on your expenses, you have more money for other purposes.

Here's what works: This month we'll focus on these action items:

· Review your total compensation statement. Your compensation goes beyond your salary to include employee benefits and retirement plan contributions.

· Review your employee benefits. Check your employee benefits to make sure that you have the right coverage to meet your needs.

· Optimize your spending. Consider ways to reduce expenses on necessary financial products and services by reviewing your options.

· Check your tax burden. While we can't adjust our tax rates, we can reduce our tax burdens with strategies such as charitable giving or contributing to retirement plans.

ON THE CALENDAR

On the monthly calendar, write in the following items:

· The month and days
· Any fixed dates
· When you're expecting income
· Any bills due this month—mark the payment date seven days prior to the due date, along with the due date
· Life events
· Items from your to-do list

To-do list:

· Action steps to take this month
· Adjustments to make
· People to talk to
· Ways to make this month great
· Things you are looking forward to this month
· Distractions to avoid

· _____

· _____

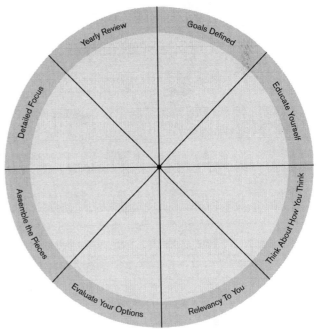

THE BOTTOM LINE

Find value so that you can minimize expenses and have more money for your other goals.

Review Your Total Compensation Statement

Sunday:

Monday:

Tuesday:

Wednesday:

Thursday:

Friday:

Saturday:

The big picture: Your total compensation includes all compensation, beyond salary.

Why it matters: When you work for a business as an owner, partner, or employee, you will typically receive compensation beyond your salary:

- Bonuses or commissions
- Health insurance, life insurance, and disability insurance
- Contributions to retirement plans
- Other benefits, such as stock incentives

What are your three big goals this week?

- Get Ready Goal: Create a total compensation statement.
- Goal 1: _____
- Goal 2: _____

Check-in: Create your total compensation statement in the table below. You can often find this information either through your company's online web portal or your annual open enrollment paperwork.

Here's what works: Your total compensation statement shows the total value of what you receive from your employer.

- Consider asking for a raise if you haven't received one in the last year.

One more thing: You can use your total compensation statement when considering a new position or venture.

Compensation Type	Value (annual)
Salary (base pay)	$
Other cash compensation (bonuses, commissions, etc.)	$
Distributions (partnership, other)	$
Insurance premiums paid by employer (usually a flex credit or lump sum for all coverages)	$
Retirement plan contributions	$
Other benefits	$
PTO accrual credit (vacation days, sick leave days, paid holidays)	_____ days
Other compensation	$
Total compensation	$

To-do list:

- Add your total compensation to the year-end summary (see week 52).
- List any changes in your life that may impact your total compensation statement.
- Write down whether you are getting paid what you're worth and whether you plan to ask for a raise.
- List who you will discuss this with.

- _____

- _____

Positive Habit Maker							
Habit	S	M	T	W	T	F	S
Goals defined							
Educate yourself							
Think about how you think							
Relevancy to you							
Evaluate your options							
Assemble the pieces							
Detailed focus							
Yearly review							

THE BOTTOM LINE

Review your total compensation statement so you can see how much you are really earning.

Review Your Employee Benefits

Sunday:	
Monday:	
Tuesday:	
Wednesday:	
Thursday:	
Friday:	
Saturday:	

The big picture: Make sure that you are taking full advantage of all of your employee benefits.

Why it matters: Whether you are an employee or an owner, it's easy to overlook some of your benefits. It's important to review them to optimize their value.

What are your three big goals this week?

- Get Ready Goal: Review your employee benefits.
- Goal 1: _____
- Goal 2: _____

Here's what works: Open enrollment is your opportunity to add or remove dependents, make changes to your group insurance, plan contributions to flexible spending accounts, and cash out some of your time off or sick leave hours, if eligible. Review the following benefits and make notes on any changes you'd like to make.

- **Disability insurance:** At open enrollment, you can increase the percentage of income covered. You can also decide if you'd like to have your disability benefits paid on a post-tax basis, which means your benefits would be paid after taxes.
- **Health insurance:** Compare premiums, deductibles, co-pays, and total out-of-pocket limits. Be aware of changes in provider networks and pharmacy benefits managers.
- **Life insurance:** Premiums for individual life insurance policies will usually be much lower for those in good health than group life insurance. Premiums are not fixed and will fluctuate.
- **Dental insurance:** Check if there is a waiting period before coverage starts and what the plan pays for, such as lab and material costs for crowns or bridges.

- **FSA and DCSA:** Plan out your contributions carefully. At open enrollment time, estimate what you will spend over the next calendar year. FSAs may allow you to carry over $500. Dependent Care Spending Accounts do not allow you to roll over any amount.

One more thing: After you enroll, be sure to review your benefit election confirmations to ensure that all of your elections and changes are correct. Benefits will generally remain in effect for the entire plan year unless you experience a qualifying change in family or employment status.

To-do list:

- List any changes in your life that will impact your employee benefits.
- List any adjustments you will be making.
- Add a reminder on your calendar to refer to this at open enrollment time.
- List who you will discuss this with.
- _____
- _____

Positive Habit Maker							
Habit	S	M	T	W	T	F	S
Goals defined							
Educate yourself							
Think about how you think							
Relevancy to you							
Evaluate your options							
Assemble the pieces							
Detailed focus							
Yearly review							

THE BOTTOM LINE

Review your employee benefits to make sure you get the full value.

Optimize Your Spending

Sunday:

Monday:

Tuesday:

Wednesday:

Thursday:

Friday:

Saturday:

The big picture: Seek value by understanding your options.
Why it matters: Finding the best value will help you reduce your expenses so that you'll have more money for your goals.

What are your three big goals this week?

- Get Ready Goal: Optimize your spending.
- Goal 1: _____
- Goal 2: _____

Check-in: Create an affordability ratio for two of the largest household expenses. The affordability ratio helps you determine how much of your income goes to these two expenses.

Auto costs:

- Step 1: Total monthly income: $_____
- Step 2: Total monthly auto costs (loan, insurance, gas, maintenance, parking, etc.): $_____
- Step 3: Divide monthly auto costs by monthly income (step 2/step 1): _____%

Housing costs:

- Step 1: Total monthly income: $_____
- Step 2: Total monthly housing costs (mortgage or rent, insurance, maintenance, property taxes): $_____
- Step 3: Divide monthly housing costs by monthly income (step 2/step 1): _____%

Your auto ratio should generally be 15 percent or lower. Your housing ratio is recommended by lenders to be 36 percent or lower.

Here's what works: To optimize your spending, be sure to understand your options and look at the details.

- Consider fees: For example, mutual fund A has an expense fee of 2 percent, and mutual fund B has an expense fee of 1 percent. Mutual fund B will save you 1 percent a year in fees, meaning that you've increased your return by 1 percent a year.
- True cost: When making a major purchase such as a car or home, calculate the total cost, which includes the price, insurance, taxes or registration, maintenance, and so on.
- Comparison shop: Do your research. If two financial products have the same benefits and one has a lower cost, opt for the lower cost.
- Insurance riders: Review your insurance policies and terminate policies and riders you don't need.
- Update coverage: Terminate products that do not meet your current goals.
- Surrender charges: If you are purchasing a new financial product, be aware of surrender charges that can impact access. A surrender charge is the amount retained by the issuer of a life insurance policy when a policy is canceled, typically assessed only during the first five to ten years of a policy.

To-do list:

- Add your auto and home affordability ratios to the year-end summary (see week 52).
- List any changes in your life that will impact how you optimize your spending.
- List any adjustments you can make.
- List who you will talk to about this.
- _____
- _____

Positive Habit Maker							
Habit	S	M	T	W	T	F	S
Goals defined							
Educate yourself							
Think about how you think							
Relevancy to you							
Evaluate your options							
Assemble the pieces							
Detailed focus							
Yearly review							

THE BOTTOM LINE

Optimizing your spending will help you lead an efficient financial life.

Check Your Tax Burden Ratio

Sunday:

Monday:

Tuesday:

Wednesday:

Thursday:

Friday:

Saturday:

The big picture: Minimizing your tax burden will help you keep more money.

Why it matters: You might be paying many types of tax, including federal income tax, state income tax, sales tax, property tax, and capital gains tax. While you have no control over the tax rate, you can use planning to reduce your tax burden.

What are your three big goals this week?

· Get Ready Goal: Check your tax burden ratio.

· Goal 1: _____

· Goal 2: _____

Check-in: Check your tax burden ratio.

· Step 1: Add up your taxes:
  ◦ Federal income tax: $_____ (IRS Form 1040, tax and credits, line 16)
  ◦ State and local income tax or general taxes: $_____ (Schedule A, part II, line 5a)
  ◦ Property tax (state and local real estate taxes): $_____ (Schedule A, part II, line 5c)
  ◦ State and local personal property taxes: $_____ (Schedule A, part II, line 5c)
  ◦ Self-employment tax: $_____ (Schedule 2, line 21)
  ◦ Total taxes: $_____
· Step 2: Gross income: $_____ (Schedule 1040, income section, line 9)
· Step 3: Tax burden ratio: $_____ (step 1/step 2)

Here's what works: Consider tax reduction strategies:

- **Adjust your charitable giving** by increasing your cash donations, especially if your income is expected to be higher; donating appreciated securities, which would offset or eliminate capital gains tax; and making qualified charitable distributions from your IRA or setting up a donor-advised fund.
- Increase your **retirement fund contributions**.
- If your property value decreases, you can usually request that your property be reassessed to possibly reduce your tax. You can use an online service like Zillow to see an estimate for your home.

One more thing: If you are using an accountant or financial advisor, they can help you spot opportunities to reduce your tax burden.

 **To-do list:**

- Add your tax burden ratio to the year-end summary (see week 52).
- List any life events that will impact your tax burden.
- List any adjustments you will be making.
- List who you will discuss this with.

- _____

- _____

Positive Habit Maker							
Habit	S	M	T	W	T	F	S
Goals defined							
Educate yourself							
Think about how you think							
Relevancy to you							
Evaluate your options							
Assemble the pieces							
Detailed focus							
Yearly review							

THE BOTTOM LINE

Reducing your tax burden will help you keep more money.

Monthly Reflection

What were your five biggest wins?

1.

2.

3.

4.

5.

ASK YOURSELF:

- How did the month go for you?
- What goals did you meet this month?
- What challenges did you overcome?
- How is your progress with the Get Ready Habits?
- How did you do with your habits?

- What were your biggest lessons learned?
- What were your insights this month?
- What tasks do you still need to work on?
- How will you improve next month?
- How will you celebrate your wins this month?

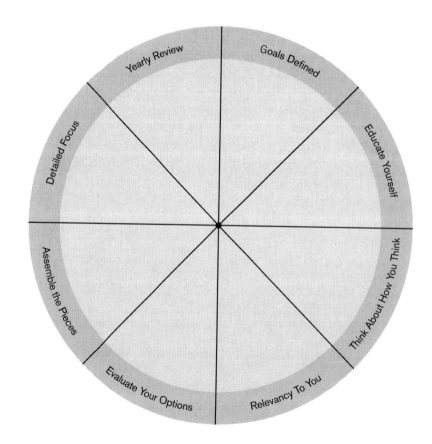

Date	Payee	Category/Purpose	Amount

Monitor Your Personal Information

MONTH 11

	Sunday	Monday	Tuesday	Wednesday	Thursday	Friday	Saturday
Week 44							
Week 45							
Week 46							
Week 47							

The big picture: Ensure that your personal information is accurate, up to date, and secure.

Why it's important: Your personal information is used to make decisions about extending credit, jobs, insurance policies, and more to you. It also dictates the interest rates that you'll pay and more. If someone gets access to your personal information, they can steal your identity.

Here's what works: This month we'll focus on these action items:

- Review your credit reports. Credit reports are used to make decisions about extending credit, jobs, and insurance policies.
- Check your credit scores. Lenders look at credit scores to decide whether to offer credit and at what interest rate.
- Order your consumer reports. Specialty consumer reporting agencies compile information on you that is used for all types of decisions such as real estate transactions and job applications.
- Protect yourself from frauds and scams. Being aware of common scams can help you stay safe.

ON THE CALENDAR

On the monthly calendar, write in the following items:

- The month and days
- Any fixed dates
- When you're expecting income
- Any bills due this month—mark the payment date seven days prior to the due date, along with the due date
- Life events
- Items from your to-do list

To-do list:

- Action steps to take this month
- Adjustments to make
- People to talk to
- Ways to make this month great
- Things you are looking forward to this month
- Distractions to avoid

- _____
- _____

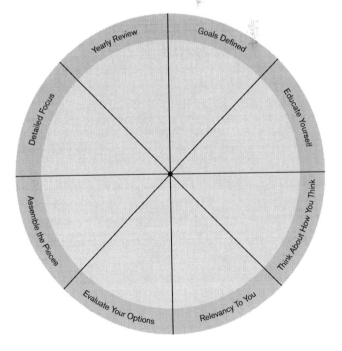

THE BOTTOM LINE

Monitoring your identity will help protect you and ensure that your personal information is accurate.

Review Your Credit Reports

Sunday:	
Monday:	
Tuesday:	
Wednesday:	
Thursday:	
Friday:	
Saturday:	

The big picture: Credit reports are used to make decisions about extending credit, jobs, and insurance policies to you.

Why it matters: Ordering your credit reports will allow you to review them for accuracy and to spot any unauthorized activity.

· Credit reports are compiled by credit reporting agencies, which collect information about where you live and work, how you pay your bills, and whether or not you have been sued, arrested, or have filed for bankruptcy.

· These companies sell your credit report to creditors, employers, insurers, and others, who will use these reports to make decisions about extending credit, jobs, and insurance policies to you.

What are your three big goals this week?

· Get Ready Goal: Review your credit report.

· Goal 1: _____

· Goal 2: _____

Check-in: Order a free copy of your credit report from each of the major credit reporting agencies (Equifax, Experian, and TransUnion) at www.annualcreditreport.com. Be careful: This website is the only one that is government authorized to provide you with free copies of your credit report. There are many sites with similar URLs that will either attempt to charge you or steal your personal information.

Here's what works: Review your credit report. You are likely the only person who can verify the accuracy of these reports.

· Check the reports to ensure they are accurate and to spot any unauthorized activity.

· Make sure that all accounts and other information listed for you on these reports is accurate and complete.

- Review account status reporting, as status and dates can be incorrect, or debts can be listed twice.
- If you find something wrong with a credit report, you can file your dispute online at each credit reporting agency's website. To do this, explain what you think is wrong in the report and provide your reasons, along with any documentation to support your case.

One more thing: You're entitled to one free report every 12 months.

To-do list:

- List any changes in your life that might impact your credit score.
- List any adjustments you will make or actions you will take.
- List who you will discuss this with.

- _____

- _____

Positive Habit Maker							
Habit	S	M	T	W	T	F	S
Goals defined							
Educate yourself							
Think about how you think							
Relevancy to you							
Evaluate your options							
Assemble the pieces							
Detailed focus							
Yearly review							

THE BOTTOM LINE

Reviewing your credit reports will help to ensure that information on your credit history is accurate and up to date.

Check Your Credit Scores

Sunday:
Monday:
Tuesday:
Wednesday:
Thursday:
Friday:
Saturday:

The big picture: Your credit scores predict how likely you are to pay back a loan on time.

Why it matters: Lenders look at your credit scores to help decide whether to offer a loan and at what interest rate. Credit scores are also used by utilities and cell phone providers.

What are your three big goals this week?

· Get Ready Goal: Check your credit scores.

· Goal 1: _____

· Goal 2: _____

Check-in: Record your credit scores.

· Credit score 1: _____ Source: _____

· Credit score 2: _____ Source: _____

What is it? According to the Consumer Financial Protection Bureau, "a credit score predicts how likely you are to pay back a loan on time. . . . Any credit score depends on the data used to calculate it, and may differ depending on the scoring model, the source of your credit history, the type of loan product, and even the day it was calculated."[1]

· Here's a breakdown of how one of the most common credit scores, the FICO Score, is calculated: payment history (35 percent), amounts owed (35 percent), length of credit history (15 percent), credit mix in use (10 percent), and new credit (10 percent) (from the Fair Isaac Corporation).

---

1 "Credit reports and scores key terms," Credit reports and scores, Consumer Financial Protection Bureau, accessed May 6, 2023, https://www.consumerfinance.gov/consumer-tools/credit-reports-and-scores/answers/key-terms/.

Here's what works: Many major credit card companies, banks, and personal finance websites offer credit scores for free, so be sure to check with the companies that handle your loans and credit cards.

- You can see a list of some of the entities that offer the Vantage Credit score on the Vantage Score's website: www.vantagescore.com/consumers/tools/free-credit-scores/.
- You can also purchase your FICO score directly from the FICO website here: www.myfico.com.

To-do list:

- Add your credit score to the year-end summary (see week 52).
- List any changes in your life that will impact your credit score, such as a new loan or late payment.
- List any adjustments you will be making.
- List who you will talk to about this.
- _____
- _____

Positive Habit Maker							
Habit	S	M	T	W	T	F	S
Goals defined							
Educate yourself							
Think about how you think							
Relevancy to you							
Evaluate your options							
Assemble the pieces							
Detailed focus							
Yearly review							

THE BOTTOM LINE

Monitoring your credit score will help you understand how you're managing debt so you can get better rates and terms.

Order Consumer Reports

Sunday:

Monday:

Tuesday:

Wednesday:

Thursday:

Friday:

Saturday:

The big picture: Make sure that information collected about you is accurate.

Why it matters: Many specialty consumer reporting companies collect and share information about your employment history, transaction history with businesses, or repayment histories for specific products or services.

· This information is used for decisions on real estate transactions, job applications, insurance applications, licenses, and more.

What are your three big goals this week?

· Get Ready Goal: Order reports from specialty consumer reporting agencies.

· Goal 1: _____

· Goal 2: _____

Here's what works: Order and review consumer reports. Here are four reports to start with:

· LexisNexis compiles information such as real estate transactions and ownership data; lien, judgment, and bankruptcy records; professional license information; and historical addresses. Request your report at https://consumer.risk.lexisnexis.com.

· The C.L.U.E. Report includes information on insurance claims histories for auto insurance and homeowners insurance. Request your report at https://consumer.risk.lexisnexis.com.

· Medical Information Bureau (MIB) records contain coded information identifying any medical conditions or medical tests reported by other MIB members for anyone who has applied for individual life insurance, disability insurance, or health insurance in the last seven years. Request your report at www.mib.com/request_your_record.html.

- The Work Number compiles employment and income information. It is used by lenders, property managers, preemployment screeners, social service agencies, and others who need to verify someone's employment status or income. Request your report at www.theworknumber.com.

One more thing: Contact the consumer reporting company to correct any incorrect information.

To-do list:

- List any changes in your life that may impact your consumer report.
- List any adjustments you need to make.
- List who you will talk to about this.
- _____
- _____

Positive Habit Maker							
Habit	S	M	T	W	T	F	S
Goals defined							
Educate yourself							
Think about how you think							
Relevancy to you							
Evaluate your options							
Assemble the pieces							
Detailed focus							
Yearly review							

THE BOTTOM LINE

You should review your consumer reports because you are likely the only person who can verify the accuracy of their information. Reviewing your information will help you with insurance premiums, job offers, and more.

Protect Yourself from Frauds and Scams

Sunday:

Monday:

Tuesday:

Wednesday:

Thursday:

Friday:

Saturday:

The big picture: Being aware can help keep you from falling prey to fraudsters.

Why it matters: Having a review system set up for all areas of your financial life will help you identify potential issues. In 2022, there were 2.4 million fraud reports for a total of $8.8 billion lost to fraud, according to the Federal Trade Commission.

What are your three big goals this week?

· Get Ready Goal: Protect yourself from frauds and scams.

· Goal 1: _____

· Goal 2: _____

Here's what works: Monitor all areas of your financial life. Look for irregularities such as unauthorized purchases on your credit cards or unexpected activities on your credit report.

· Set unique and hard-to-guess passwords or use phrases that can be harder to guess, like GetReady&StayPrepared1. You can use a password manager (Apple products have a password manager built in).

· Shred documents with personal information.

· Review your bank and credit card statements monthly. Contact your bank or credit card company if you notice suspicious activity.

· Order and review your credit reports.

· Add a security freeze on your credit report, which prevents new creditors from accessing your credit file and others from opening accounts in your name until you lift the freeze.

· When using public Wi-Fi or an unsecured network, don't use any personal information or log in to any websites.

- Be wary of unknown calls and texts.
- Review health insurance explanation-of-benefits statements to avoid medical identity fraud.
- Use two-factor authentication whenever possible.
- Do not respond to phone calls, texts, or emails from the IRS or Social Security. They will not call, text, or email you.
- If any communication seems fishy, check with the official, publicly available phone number.
- If it's too good to be true, it probably is.

To-do list:

- List any changes in your life that may create an opportunity for a fraudster.
- List any adjustments you will be making.
- List who you will discuss this with.

- _____

- _____

Positive Habit Maker							
Habit	S	M	T	W	T	F	S
Goals defined							
Educate yourself							
Think about how you think							
Relevancy to you							
Evaluate your options							
Assemble the pieces							
Detailed focus							
Yearly review							

THE BOTTOM LINE

Monitoring your financial life is essential to protecting your money.

Monthly Reflection

What were your five biggest wins?

1.

2.

3.

4.

5.

ASK YOURSELF:

- How did the month go for you?
- What goals did you meet this month?
- What challenges did you overcome?
- How is your progress with the Get Ready Habits?
- How did you do with your habits?

- What were your biggest lessons learned?
- What were your insights this month?
- What tasks do you still need to work on?
- How will you improve next month?
- How will you celebrate your wins this month?

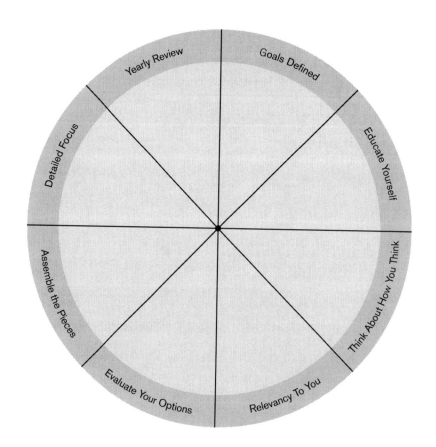

Expense Tracker

Date	Payee	Category/Purpose	Amount

Wrap Up Loose Ends

MONTH 12

	Sunday	Monday	Tuesday	Wednesday	Thursday	Friday	Saturday
Week 48							
Week 49							
Week 50							
Week 51							
Week 52							

The big picture: There's always something that ends up not getting attended to.

Why it's important: Taking care of the loose ends helps you make sure that you keep everything up to date.

Here's what works: This month we'll focus on these action items:

- Review your charitable giving. Maximize your charitable giving with a strategy.
- Search for unclaimed property. With over $42 billion in unclaimed property, there's a good chance that some of it may be yours.
- Review end-of-year items. Be sure to meet end-of-year items to have a positive impact on your financial life.
- Be mindful of money myths. Being able to separate fact from fiction will help you choose the products and services that best fit your needs.

ON THE CALENDAR

On the monthly calendar, write in the following items:

- The month and days
- Any fixed dates
- When you're expecting income
- Any bills due this month—mark the payment date seven days prior to the due date, along with the due date
- Life events
- Items from your to-do list

 **To-do list:**

- Action steps to take this month
- Adjustments to make
- People to talk to
- Ways to make this month great
- Things you are looking forward to this month
- Distractions to avoid

- _____
- _____

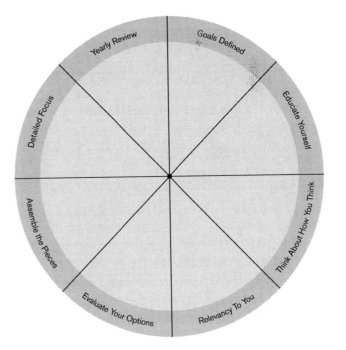

THE BOTTOM LINE

Wrap up loose ends to keep everything on track.

Review Your Charitable Giving Strategy

Sunday:

Monday:

Tuesday:

Wednesday:

Thursday:

Friday:

Saturday:

The big picture: Charitable giving can be a significant portion of our expenses.

Why it matters: Giving to charities is an essential part of our lives. Americans gave $484.85 billion to charities in 2021, and six out of ten American households participate in some sort of charitable giving, according to the Philanthropy Roundtable.

What are your three big goals this week?

· Get Ready Goal: Review your charitable giving strategy.

· Goal 1: _____

· Goal 2: _____

Check-in: Calculate your charitable giving ratio. This ratio shows how much of your income goes to charity.

· Step 1: Adjusted gross income: $_____ (you can find this on your most recent tax return)

· Step 2: Annual charitable donations: $_____

· Step 3: Divide adjusted gross income by charitable donations (step1/step2): _____ %

Here's what works: Create a strategy for your charitable giving.

· Add your estimated annual giving to your cash flow worksheet and to your budget (if you have one). Make sure that you have the money to donate; cover your expenses and savings goals first.

· Consider what causes are important to you. Prioritize the causes since you may not be able to give to all of them.

· Research the causes and which nonprofits are active in your area. Consider how they make an impact, how they will use your donation, how much of your donation goes to programs, along with their mission and activities.

- Check that the fundraiser and charity are registered with your state's charity regulator (www .nasconet.org/resources/state-government).
- These organizations can help you research a charity: Charity Navigator (www.charitynavigator.org), BBB Wise Giving Alliance (www.give.org), and Charity Watch (www.charitywatch.org).
- Check the organization's tax-exempt status on the IRS website (www.irs.gov/charities-non-profits/ tax-exempt-organization-search).
- Keep a written record of all donations for tax purposes.
- Be alert for scams. If giving online, check that it's the nonprofit's official website and that it's a secure connection (look for *https* in the web address).

One more thing: Cash donations are just the start of how you can give money to charities. You can work with a nonprofit's planned giving officer for larger gifts that can include investments and property. You can also set up a donor-advised fund, which allows donors to make contributions to the charity, become eligible to take an immediate tax deduction, and then make recommendations on distributing the funds to qualified charitable organizations.

To-do list:

- Add your charitable giving ratio to the year-end summary (see week 52).
- List any changes in your life that may impact your charitable giving.
- List any adjustments you will be making.
- List any advisors you will be talking to about this.

- _____
- _____

Positive Habit Maker							
Habit	S	M	T	W	T	F	S
Goals defined							
Educate yourself							
Think about how you think							
Relevancy to you							
Evaluate your options							
Assemble the pieces							
Detailed focus							
Yearly review							

THE BOTTOM LINE

With research and planning, giving is a great way to make an impact with the causes that are important to you.

Search for Unclaimed Property

Sunday:	
Monday:	
Tuesday:	
Wednesday:	
Thursday:	
Friday:	
Saturday:	

The big picture: There are many free and easy ways to search to see if you have unclaimed money.

Why it matters: States are currently holding approximately $42 billion in unclaimed property from abandoned bank accounts, safe deposit box contents, stocks, uncashed dividend or payroll checks, bonds, mutual funds, and utility security deposits, according to the National Association of Unclaimed Property Administrators (NAUPA).

What are your three big goals this week?

· Get Ready Goal: Search for unclaimed property.

· Goal 1: _____

· Goal 2: _____

Here's what works: There are many free and easy ways to search to see if you have unclaimed money.

· NAUPA's website has more information and links to your state's unclaimed property website. Visit www.unclaimed.org.

· NAUPA and participating states and provinces have officially endorsed Missing Money (www.missingmoney.com). On their site, you can search all participating states to find your family's missing, lost, and unclaimed property, money, and assets.

· Searches and claims are always free on both sites.

· If you find unclaimed property, you'll need to file a claim. Each source will have its own procedure, so be sure to read the instructions carefully.

One more thing: These services are free for both searching and claiming. You will not ever be required to pay any type of fee. Companies may offer to find this money for a fee. And scammers may try to trick you with fake promises of money from the government or other sources.

To-do list:

· List any life events that might lead to unclaimed property.

· List any adjustments you will be making.

· List who you will discuss this with.

· _____

· _____

Positive Habit Maker							
Habit	S	M	T	W	T	F	S
Goals defined							
Educate yourself							
Think about how you think							
Relevancy to you							
Evaluate your options							
Assemble the pieces							
Detailed focus							
Yearly review							

THE BOTTOM LINE

With $42 billion in unclaimed property, there's a good chance that you'll find some missing money.

Review End-of-Year Items

Sunday:
Monday:
Tuesday:
Wednesday:
Thursday:
Friday:
Saturday:

The big picture: At the end of the year, there are important money deadlines.

Why it matters: Meeting end-of-year deadlines can have a significant positive impact on your financial life.

What are your three big goals this week?

- Get Ready Goal: Review end-of-year items.
- Goal 1: _____
- Goal 2: _____

Here's what works: Keep an eye on your holiday budget. While using credit cards is a great way to earn cash back or rewards, you'll need to be sure that you can pay off the balance with your next statement so you can avoid high interest charges.

- Review your spending account balances. Dependent Care Spending Accounts (DCSAs) and many Flexible Spending Accounts (FSAs) have a "use it or lose it" policy. If you will have money left over, here are some applicable expenses for FSAs: vision (new glasses or contacts), chiropractic care, acupuncture, prescription medications, and mental health treatment (therapy). Learn more on the IRS site at www.irs.gov.

- Make any year-end charitable donations to support your favorite nonprofits to make a positive difference and to be able to claim your tax deduction. Be sure to check whether your donation is tax deductible.

- Complete any gifts to people or trusts to take advantage of the annual gift tax exclusion. The annual gift tax exclusion limits increase each year.

- Review your IRA and 401(k) contributions and distributions. If you had to take a first required minimum distribution by April 1, you must take your second by December 31.
- Medicare open enrollment typically ends on December 7. Open enrollment is generally the only time of year when you can make changes to your Medicare plans. Changes made during this period go into effect January 1 of the next year. Learn more at www.medicare.gov.

One more thing: Use your gift cards. Consider gifting any that you won't be using to your family and friends. Or you can sell them; although you'll get less than face value, you'll have something.

 **To-do list:**

- List any changes in your life that will impact these end-of-year deadlines.
- List any adjustments you will be making.
- List who you will discuss this with.

- _____

- _____

Positive Habit Maker							
Habit	S	M	T	W	T	F	S
Goals defined							
Educate yourself							
Think about how you think							
Relevancy to you							
Evaluate your options							
Assemble the pieces							
Detailed focus							
Yearly review							

THE BOTTOM LINE

Reviewing and completing end-of-year items will help you maximize your financial life.

Be Mindful of These Money Myths

Sunday:	
Monday:	
Tuesday:	
Wednesday:	
Thursday:	
Friday:	
Saturday:	

The big picture: There are many common money myths to avoid.

Why it matters: Being able to separate fact from fiction will help you choose the products and services that best fit your needs.

What are your goals this week?

· Get Ready Goal: Be mindful of money myths.

· Goal 1: _____

· Goal 2: _____

Here's what works: Following are some common money myths and what you should know:

· Myth: *Debt is bad.* Debt allows you to use other people's money. The key with debt is that the interest rate should be lower than your potential return with other uses of your money. Your monthly debt interest should fit within your cash flow, and your projected investment return should be conservative and allow for volatility. If you have a mortgage with a low interest rate, you will most likely be able to earn more by investing while being able to deduct the interest.

· Myth: *Go with the lowest cost.* While on the surface, this can often hold true, there can be many reasons why you should go deeper than price. The return may not be as good, there may be higher fees, or the company may not be as solid. Do your research and make sure that you're comparing apples to apples.

· Myth: *I am young, so I don't need to save yet.* The earlier you start, the better. This is due to the magic of compound interest. The longer you wait to start to invest, the more you'll have to put aside to have the same amount.

COMPOUND INTEREST

Compound interest is the interest you earn on interest. If you have $100 and it earns 5 percent interest each year, you'll have $105 at the end of the first year. At the end of the second year, you'll have $110.25. Not only did you earn $5 on the initial $100 deposit, you also earned $0.25 on the $5 in interest.

But the effect of compound interest grows over time. Let's say Jane starts investing $7,000 a year at age 35 and earns 7 percent per year; she has a total of $707,511 at age 65. John starts ten years later, at age 45, invests $15,500 per year, and earns the same 7 percent per year; he ends up with $657,948 at age 65. Jane's total contributions of $210,000 are $90,000 less than John's total contributions of $300,000, but she has $49,563 more in her account.

- Myth: *It's too late to start.* It's never too late to start. Even small steps will help you on your journey to financial preparedness.
- Myth: *I have a high income, so I don't need to worry about spending.* Beware of lifestyle creep. Rather than buying a newer and bigger house and pricier car, put money aside into savings first.
- Myth: *Investing is for the rich.* Investing is for everyone. You can start investing with very small amounts of money with traditional brokerages like Schwab, Vanguard, and Fidelity or with robo-advisors or apps. A great place to start out is with your employer's 401(k) or 403(b) plan if they offer one. Do your research, compare fees, and remember that this is your money and your choice.

To-do list:

- List any adjustments you need to make.
- List who you will discuss this with.
- _____
- _____

Positive Habit Maker							
Habit	S	M	T	W	T	F	S
Goals defined							
Educate yourself							
Think about how you think							
Relevancy to you							
Evaluate your options							
Assemble the pieces							
Detailed focus							
Yearly review							

THE BOTTOM LINE

Being mindful of common money myths helps you make smarter choices.

Year-End Summary

Your name: _____ Phone number: _____

Email address: _____

Emergency contact name: _____ Phone number: _____

Email address: _____

Spouse/domestic partner name: _____ Phone number: _____

Email address: _____

Child name: _____ Phone number: _____

Email address: _____

Child name: _____ Phone number: _____

Email address: _____

Parent name: _____ Phone number: _____

Email address: _____

Parent name: _____ Phone number: _____

Email address: _____

Health care agent: _____ Phone number: _____

Email address: _____

Power of attorney: _____ Phone number: _____

Email address: _____

Executor: _____ Phone number: _____

Email address: _____

Trustee: _____ Phone number: _____

Email address: _____

Guardian name: _____ Phone number: _____

Email address: _____

Employer contact: _____ Phone number: _____

Email address: _____

Employer benefits contact: _____ Phone number: _____

Email address: _____

Other: _____ Phone number: _____

Email address: _____

Other: _____ Phone number: _____

Email address: _____

Other: _____ Phone number: _____

Email address: _____

ADVISORS

Accountant (CPA)/bookkeeper/tax professional: _____

Phone number: _____ Email address: _____

Estate planning attorney: _____ Phone number: _____

Email address: _____

Financial planner: _____ Phone number: _____

Email address: _____

Financial coach: _____ Phone number: _____

Email address: _____

Financial therapist: _____ Phone number: _____

Email address: _____

Insurance agent (auto): _____ Phone number: _____

Email address: _____

Insurance agent (disability): _____ Phone number: _____

Email address: _____

Insurance agent (home): _____ Phone number: _____

Email address: _____

Insurance agent (health/Medicare): _____ Phone number: _____

Email address: _____

Other: _____ Phone number: _____

Email address: _____

Other: _____ Phone number: _____

Email address: _____

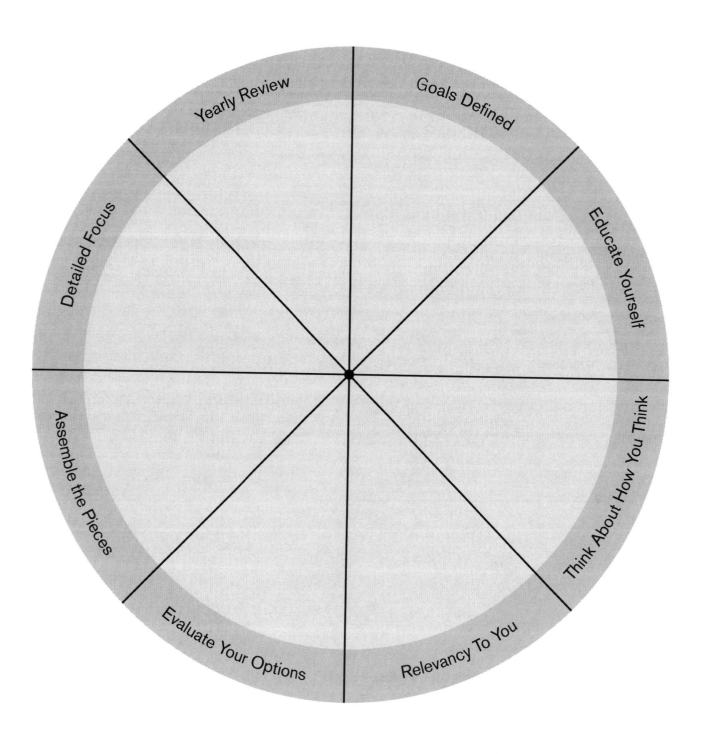

Big three goals and priorities for the year (SMART + priority) (from week 2):

- Goal 1: _____
- Goal 2: _____
- Goal 3: _____

YOUR NUMBERS

- Your life stage this year: _____ (from week 3)
- Life events this year: _____ (from week 4)
- The central location for your documents: _____ (from week 5)
- Home inventory location/storage app or website, such as iCloud: _____ (from week 7)
- Total income: $_____ (from week 14)
- Total expenses: $_____ (from week 15)
- Net cash flow: $_____ (from week 16)
- Budget ratio: _____ (from week 17)
- Property and assets total fair-market value: $_____ (from week 19)
- Debt-to-income ratio: _____ (from week 20)
- Net worth: $_____ (from week 21)
- Net worth ratio: _____ (from week 21)
- Savings ratio: _____ (from week 22)
- Liquidity ratio: _____ (rainy day fund—from week 23)
- Disability insurance ratio: _____ (from week 30)
- Estate planning documents location: _____ (from week 32)
- Powers of attorney and directives location: _____ (from week 33)
- Life insurance ratio: _____ (from week 34)
- Retirement plans balance: $_____ (from week 36)
- Passive income ratio: _____ (from week 37)
- Financial independence ratio: _____ (from week 38)
- Total compensation: $_____ (from week 40)
- Auto affordability ratio: _____ (from week 42)
- Home affordability ratio: _____ (from week 42)
- Tax burden ratio: _____ (from week 43)
- Credit score: _____ Source: _____ (from week 45)
- Charitable giving ratio: _____ (from week 48)

Monthly Reflection

What were your five biggest wins?

1.

2.

3.

4.

5.

ASK YOURSELF:

- How did the month go for you?
- What goals did you meet this month?
- What challenges did you overcome?
- How is your progress with the Get Ready Habits?
- How did you do with your habits?

- What were your biggest lessons learned?
- What were your insights this month?
- What tasks do you still need to work on?
- How will you improve next month?
- How will you celebrate your wins this month?

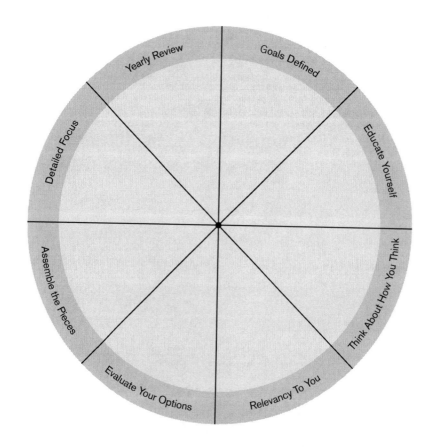

Expense Tracker

Date	Payee	Category/Purpose	Amount

NOTES

NOTES

NOTES

NOTES

✏️ NOTES

NOTES

NOTES

NOTES

Become a Get Ready Insider

The Get Ready Insider Program is a step-by-step system to help you get ready and stay prepared. It is based on eight habits that will empower you with your money and transform your life. The program includes an innovative and unique financial calendar system that provides the weekly action items (from this book) to help you stay on track and keep all areas of your financial life up to date.

The Get Ready Insider Program will help you

- learn healthy money habits to take control of your financial life,
- organize your financial life, and
- become fully empowered with your money so you can live the life you dream of.

As a Get Ready Insider, you'll receive access to the following:

- The Get Ready 52 weekly action item emails (Over 52 weeks, you'll receive a Weekly Accountability email with the action items from this book.)
- *The Get Ready! Blueprint* (fillable PDF version)
- The Get Ready Toolkit (100+ worksheets)
- Investment Policy Statement template
- Unclaimed property search worksheet
- Get Ready Movement Leader Kit: tools for clubs, masterminds, and teams

Learn more at www.tonysteuer.com.

Tony Steuer—Bookshelf Special Offer

As a thank-you to my readers, you can receive 20 percent off digital versions of all my books when purchased from my website (www.tonysteuer.com) with coupon code GETREADYBLUEPRINT20.

The Get Ready! Blueprint is a 52-week guide to changing the way you think about money—an innovative/interactive workbook with an easy-to-use, step-by-step system to help you get useful tips on all areas of your financial life.

Get Ready! shows you how to organize your financial life with a comprehensive, easy-to-follow, step-by-step process. *Get Ready!* explains every component of your financial life.

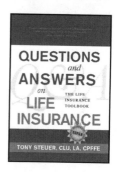

Questions and Answers on Life Insurance covers all the basics and advanced information that you need to know to understand life insurance.

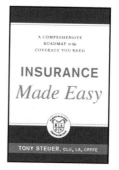

Insurance Made Easy is a comprehensive guide to insurance—from how to calculate your ideal level of coverage, to choosing a policy, to ways to save money.

The Questions and Answers on Insurance Planner covers basic buying and monitoring information for life, health, disability, long-term care, annuity, and auto insurance.

The Questions and Answers on Life Insurance Workbook is a step-by-step workbook that leads you through the process of purchasing a new life insurance policy and monitoring an existing policy.

The Questions and Answers on Disability Insurance Workbook is a step-by-step workbook that leads you through the process of purchasing a disability insurance policy and monitoring an existing policy.

A Note from the Author

Dear Reader,

Thank you for checking out *The Get Ready! Blueprint*. I hope that you feel in control and empowered with your money.

Healthy money habits help you understand all areas of your financial life and how they fit together. Being able to ask the right questions will bring you success in meeting your goals and understanding how everything fits together.

If you loved the book and have a minute to spare, I would really appreciate a short review on your favorite book site. You're the reason why I continue to write about changing the way we think about money through financial preparedness and advocating for integrity in financial services.

If you think this book might help a family member or friend with their own money, feel free to invite them to join the Get Ready Movement at www.tonysteuer.com. They'll receive the Get Ready Roadmap as well as helpful tips for reviewing all aspects of their money.

So what's next? Join the Get Ready Movement and stay up to date on the latest in changing the way we think about money by subscribing to the Get Ready! Newsletter and joining our community.

Cheers,

Tony

P.S. Listen to *The Get Ready Money Podcast*: Change the way you think about money. It includes insightful conversations with thought leaders that will provide you with practical advice that demystifies the complexities of finance and helps you build healthy habits that actually work.

P.S.S. If you are passionate about helping people feel empowered with their money, then please join the Get Ready! Expert Money Guides: Dedicated to Helping People Change the Way They Think about Money group on LinkedIn.

About the Author

TONY STEUER, CLU, LA, CPFFE is an internationally recognized financial preparedness advocate, award-winning author, and podcaster. Known as a trailblazer in financial wellness, Tony's mission is to change the way we think about money.

Tony is the creator of the Get Ready Method, which is an easy-to-use roadmap to help you understand how everything fits together. It's based on eight habits that will empower you with money and transform your life. It includes an innovative and unique financial calendar system that provides a weekly action item to help you stay on track and keep all areas of your financial life up to date.

Tony is also an advisor at Paperwork and Dingo Technologies. He is a contributor to Forbes Advisor, as well as an expert content reviewer for NerdWallet. Tony is a member of Think Advisor's LUMINARIES class of 2022 as a finalist in Thought Leadership & Education. Tony served as a long-term member of the California Department of Insurance Curriculum Board.

Tony regularly consults with fintechs, financial planners, insurance agencies, attorneys, insurance companies, and other financial service companies on financial preparedness, insurance marketing, product best practices, and best practices. Tony is a past member of the National Financial Educator's Council (NFEC) Curriculum Advisory Board.

Tony is regularly featured in the media as an expert source, including ABC's *Seven on Your Side*, *Forbes*, NerdWallet, Cheddar TV, the *New York Times*, the *Washington Post*, *Fast Company*, the *Chicago Tribune*, CNBC, and Fox Business News. Tony is also a frequent guest on podcasts. Tony also served as a technical editor for The Retirement Bible and The Investing Bible.

He is passionate about giving back. Tony is involved with many worthwhile causes, including CLCS (Community Learning Center Schools—vice president) and JDRF (Juvenile Diabetes Research Foundation—volunteer), and has served on multiple boards and advisory committees. Tony has also been a coach for his son's basketball team and baseball teams, taught wilderness first aid and white-water rescue, volunteered as a white-water raft guide, and performed improvisational comedy.

Tony Steuer lives in Alameda, California.

Made in the USA
Middletown, DE
02 November 2023

41823653R00124